A STUDIO PRESS BOOK

First published in the UK in 2024 by Studio Press,
an imprint of Bonnier Books UK,
4th Floor, Victoria House, Bloomsbury Square,
London WC1B 4DA
Owned by Bonnier Books, Sveavägen 56, Stockholm, Sweden

www.bonnierbooks.co.uk

1 3 5 7 9 10 8 6 4 2

All rights reserved
ISBN 978-1-80078-957-9

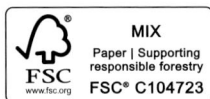

FSC
www.fsc.org

MIX
Paper | Supporting
responsible forestry
FSC® C104723

Written by Rachael Taylor
Edited by Stephanie Milton
Designed by Maddox Philpot
Picture Research by Paul Ashman
Production by Giulia Caparrelli

A CIP catalogue record for this book
is available from the British Library

Printed and bound in China

The publisher would like to thank the following for supplying photos for
this book: Alamy, Bridgeman Images, Bulgari, Getty, Shutterstock and Sotheby's.
Every effort has been made to obtain permission to reproduce copyright material
but there may be cases where we have not been able to trace a copyright holder.
The publisher will be happy to correct any omissions in future printing.

BVLGARI

The Story Behind the Style

RACHAEL TAYLOR

Contents

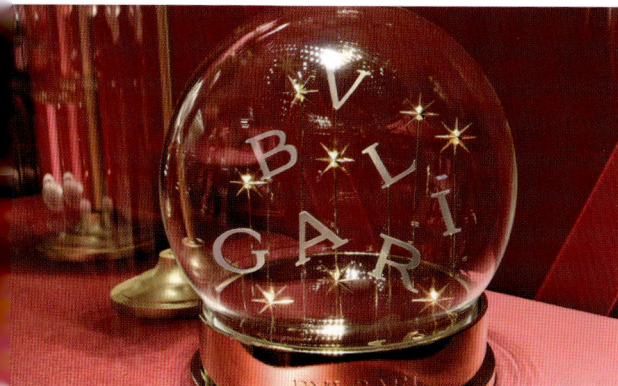

LEFT: A snow globe-inspired window display at the Bulgari store on Via dei Condotti, Rome.

Bulgari

To covet Bulgari is to covet life, in all its glorious technicolour. It is a wish to embrace exuberance and throw caution to the wind. This is the singular allure of Italy's most famous – and most colourful – jeweller.

The company, which for more than a century was controlled by one charismatic family, rose to global fame in Rome's La Dolce Vita era, when Hollywood flocked to the Eternal City. The stars found the Bulgaris ready and waiting on Via Condotti, with a selection of jewels as bold as the times. Soon, word spread. For those seeking to stand out, Bulgari became the place to go; be it for its colourful cabochon gems or the provocative coils of its Serpenti watches.

A spirit of adventure has defined the Bulgari story, starting with a young man's desire to see the world which prompted him to travel from Greece to Italy. And it has continued with pioneering future generations seeking new ways of designing – and, in doing so, developing Bulgari's distinctive jewellery style, as well as some record-breaking watches. Today, the Bvlgari branding is a common sight on the world's best shopping streets, and on its growing network of hotels. The moniker is a reliable signum of luxury and decadence. But every story has to start somewhere. This powerhouse of luxury had humble beginnings, and it is testament to the passionate personalities within the Bulgari family that a small shop in Rome that catered to tourists flourished and grew into one of the world's leading luxury lights.

PREVIOUS: The entrance to Bulgari's boutique in the centre of Florence, Italy.

TOP: Bulgari founder Sotirio Voulgaris.

ABOVE: The first S. Bulgari store opened in 1884.

Early History

Sotirio Voulgaris is the founder of the most famous Italian jewellery brand of all time, yet his story does not start in Italy. It begins in Greece.

Sotirio was born on 18th March, 1857, in Paramythia, a small town in northern Greece that lies about 100km from the Albanian border. He was one of 11 children born to Georgis and Eleni Voulgaris, but, sadly, was the only one to survive. It seems that destiny touched the future jeweller from an early age.

Georgis Voulgaris was a skilled silversmith who had grown up in Kalarrytes, which at the time, was the largest silversmithing centre in the Balkans. Georgis' father had also been a silversmith, and had introduced him to the business. When it came time for his own son, Sotirio, to learn the trade, it was natural for Georgis to take him under his wing. With his father's steady guidance, the young Sotirio learned how to craft belts, earrings, sword sheaths and buttons, all made out of silver.

The family had a store in Paramythia from which they sold their goods. It should have been a safe and steady life, but the Voulgaris lived in an era of political tension. In 1878, the Epirus region, of which Paramythia was a part, was taken under Ottoman rule, and tensions were high between Turks and Greeks. A series of arson attacks took place to target Greek businesses, during which the Voulgaris' shop was set ablaze. Eventually, the entire village of Paramythia was burned to the ground – a purposeful move by its leaders so that the town could be rebuilt from scratch. The Voulgaris family, however, did not stick around for this promised new era. They left Paramythia, with Eleni moving in with relatives in Albania, and Sotirio and Georgis embarking on a nomadic life that never allowed them to spend more than a month in one place.

The Voulgaris family continued to make and sell silverware during this time, but life on the road was dangerous. The winters in the mountains were bitterly cold, and they would often require protection from soldiers to transport their expensive goods from town to town.

In 1876, when Sotirio was 18 years old, he fell victim to an attempted robbery; it was the beginning of the end of his days as a travelling salesman. The following year, he and his father left the mainland and set up home on the island of Corfu. There, they opened a small workshop on the ground floor of a house. Once they were settled, Eleni joined them, and the family was soon immersed in the life of the island.

During his time in Corfu, Sotirio made a friend that would prove to be a catalyst for the next part of his life, a Macedonian silversmith called Demetrio Kremos. Things were going well for his family in Corfu, but young Sotirio felt restless, and Demetrio offered a solution. The Macedonian was on his way to Italy and persuaded Sotirio to join him.

In the autumn of 1880, the friends set sail for Brindisi, a port city on the very heel of Italy that faces out into the Adriatic Sea. From there, they travelled across the country to Naples, where the budding entrepreneurs set about building their fortune.

Both were skilled silversmiths, and they pooled their talent to open a store in Naples' Piazza dei Martiri, a town square known for silverware sellers. It was the perfect landing spot.

This good fortune didn't last, however. One night when the business partners were out at dinner, the shop was broken into, and much of their stock was stolen. This led to them closing the Naples shop, and setting their sights on new beginnings in Rome.

On 18th February, 1881, Sotirio and Demetrio arrived in the 'Eternal City'. Sortirio was 23 years old, and – following the robbery at his shop – had just 80 centesimi in his

ABOVE: The Old Curiosity Shop on Via Condotti in Rome targeted tourists to the city.

pocket. Pulling together what goods they had left, the pair started trading from a stall in front of the French Academy art gallery. The only problem was, they didn't have a licence. They were caught and shut down by the authorities within three days, but the reward had been worth the risk. During that time, they had managed to make 200 lira. With the funds they had raised, they managed to set up a more legitimate business – a store at 75 Via Sistina. It would be a short-lived partnership, however.

Unfortunately, just as in Naples, the dream would be short lived. This time, the turmoil came from within, with the friends falling out over money, and parting ways.

Sotirio's relationship with Via Sistina wasn't quite over, however. He liked the street. It was populated by other Greek silversmiths, as well as other types of craftspeople and some art shops. He felt it was the right spot for him, and in 1884 he opened a store at 85 Via Sistina under his own name – well, almost. The trading name of the shop was S. Bulgari, an Italianised spelling of his last name chosen to help shoppers better pronounce Voulgaris.

Sotirio filled his store with silverware – salvers, spoons, goblets, belt buckles and chatelains. This mish-mash of silver attracted tourists visiting Rome. The city was a key destination at that time for European and American tourists embarking on so-called Grand Tours.

Four years after setting up S. Bulgari in Rome, Sotirio got married. Rather than a romantic Italian love affair, the union was a Greek arranged marriage. His bride, Eleni Basios, was the daughter of his parents' neighbours in Corfu, and was just 17 years old when they wed. Eleni and Sotirio would go on to have six children together, all of whom were brought up in Rome. Constantino Giorgio was born in 1889, followed a year later by Giorgio Leonida and Maria Athena the year after that. In 1893, Sophia arrived and her sister Alexandra was born two years later. Then the couple was blessed with a final son, Spiridione, in 1897. The family would be known by the Bulgari surname.

ABOVE: A mid-19th century gold, emerald, and enamel bracelet sold by S. Bulgari, which sold for CHF27,400 at Sotheby's in 2007.

Early expansion

The original S. Bulgari store at 85 Via Sistina would remain open for nearly 40 years, but it was far from Sotirio's only retail venture. In 1894, a second S. Bulgari store opened at 28 Via Condotti. Similarly, this was filled with middle-of-the-range antiques, silver and curiosities, with its window displays packed with hundreds of items to lure passers-by. A line in French – the most fashionable language of the time – proclaimed its wares to be: bijoux, argenteria artistica, antiquities, curiosities.

The jeweller also looked beyond landlocked Rome to various holiday destinations, prompted by the city's quiet streets at the height of summer. A store was opened in coastal Naples, as well as in the Swiss holiday resorts of St-Moritz-Bad and Lucerne. More locations followed in the final five years of the 19th century, including San Remo, Bellagio and Sorrento.

Then, in 1905, came a very special opening at 10 Via Condotti in Rome. As there was already an S. Bulgari store on this street, Sortirio gave this one a rather quaint name – The Old Curiosity Shop. Naming it after a Charles Dickens novel was a nod to the English-speaking tourists that made up much of his business,

as well as an indication of the type of stock it carried and the clientele it catered to. The Bulgari of the turn of the 20th century was very different to what it would later become.

Sotirio was immensely proud of his empire of stores, but as the business began to pivot, and quality jewels and silverware started to play a more important role, he knew that he needed to narrow his focus. Thus, he began to reduce his network of stores by closing them or giving them to family members to run, making way for Bulgari to evolve into a luxury business.

OPPOSITE: A view down Via Condotti, looking towards Rome's Piazza di Spagna, circa 1915.

ABOVE: Holidaymakers ice skate at St Moritz, Switzerland, in 1905.

Silver

The Bulgari story is steeped in silver. From the long line of Voulgaris silversmiths in Greece to the windows of The Curiosity Shop, it is part of the brand's DNA. Today, you might be more likely to associate Bulgari with an emerald necklace, but historically it would have been somewhere to buy a spoon or a belt buckle, as well as more elaborate examples of silverware.

Early pieces of Bulgari silver would have been produced in an alloy known as 800 silver – made up of 80 per cent pure silver and 20 per cent other metals, such as copper or zinc. This is a lower quality than the 925 (92.5 per cent pure) silver that is used today, but 800 silver was the common standard in Italy at that time.

By 1900, Sotirio started to collect antique European silverware made by other makers, amassing an impressive archive. He passed his passion for silverware on to his son Constantino Bulgari, who started his own collecting journey in the late 1920s. Constantino would go on to dedicate his life to the study of silver and hallmarks (the marks that are struck on precious metal to authenticate it, as well as credit a design to locations and makers). He would go on to write Argentieri *Gemmari e Orafi d'Italia*, a five-volume history of Italian hallmarks. The books were published between 1958 and 1974, the year after Constantino died. They were considered to be a highly authoritative work, and would have been incredibly complex to research as, historically, Italy had been divided into different regions and kingdoms, each with its own laws.

Constantino was also in touch with international hallmarking bodies and worked with The Goldsmiths' Company in London to register SB as a maker's mark for Sortirio Bulgari. At the time, Bulgari was the only non-British company to have a maker's mark registered there. You will find the SB mark on all Bulgari silverware.

Constantino, in turn, shared his passion for silver with his nephew Nicola Bulgari, with whom he was very close. Nicola's interest led to silverware remaining a core part of the Bulgari business. In 1979, the brand started to produce contemporary silver homeware objects, such as ashtrays,

ABOVE: A silver tureen showing the 'SB' hallmark for Sotirio Bulgari, circa 1993, and sold for €4,410 at Sotheby's in 2021.

coffee pots, book ends and money clips. The first collection was called Colonna (column) and was defined by sleek contours, rounded edges, volume and substantial weight. In 1988, Bulgari travelled to London to take part in an exhibition of silverware at the Goldsmiths' Hall, and worked with The Goldsmiths' Company to sponsor young

OPPOSITE: A silver cigarette box mounted with ancient Roman coins, crafted by Bulgari in 1969, and sold for US$9,375 at Sotheby's in 2010 as part of the collection of socialite Patricia Kluge.

silversmiths. Another London fair beckoned in 1991. This time it was the Grosvenor House Antique Fair, at which Bulgari showcased some of the antique silverware that three generations of the family had collected. The fair was visited by the Queen Mother, who made a point of noting her interest in Bulgari's display.

Today, Bulgari outsources its silversmithing, but still makes many interesting and unusual pieces. As Nicola Bulgari told *Architectural Digest* in 2009: "Our clients can ask us to make anything for them in silver. We've made scale models of yachts and even buildings – as well as one very fine roulette wheel. We've worked closely with the same family of silversmiths, so they are now well used to unusual requests."

Becoming Bulgari

The Bulgari of today is very different to the company that Sotirio first created. While it had found success with its silver trinkets for tourists, it would start to forge a new identity for itself at the dawn of the 20th century – one that would position it as a serious player in luxury jewels.

Much of the change would be driven by the arrival in the business of the jeweller's sons, Giorgio and Constantino. Together, they would usher in a new era for the jeweller that would see it offer ever-larger gemstones, on-trend high jewels crafted with complex techniques, and some new and innovative designs that were unique to Bulgari.

LEFT: A gold, diamond, sapphire and emerald Serpenti necklace in a Bulgari store window in Milan.

Giorgio & Constantino

Sotirio had six children, but it was his two eldest sons, Constantino and Giorgio, to whom he would entrust his legacy. The brothers, who were born a year apart, joined the family business as teenagers. Their induction into the world of jewellery came at a precarious time for the business as World War I practically brought it to a standstill, but the Bulgaris kept the stores afloat.

When Sotirio died in 1932, at the age of 75, the business passed to Constantino and Giorgio. The brothers would make their own mark on the brand, and the wider jewellery world, with each bringing something very different to the table. Constantino, the eldest, had a strong interest in silversmithing and academic study. Giorgio, meanwhile, found his passion lay in jewellery and gemstones, and he would be instrumental in the transformation of the business from purveyor of tourist trinkets to maker of some of the world's most luxurious jewels.

Both brothers were well liked and had a reputation for kindness. During World War II, Constantino and his wife Laura risked their lives to hide three Jewish women in their home. The women had knocked on the Bulgaris' door seeking sanctuary during the 1943 raid on Rome's ghetto that led to 1,000 Jews being rounded up and sent to concentration camps. The Bulgari family was also known to assist Allied troops, even though Italy did not switch sides until 1943.

OPPOSITE: Sotirio, Giorgio and Leonilde Bulgari. Leonilde was Giorgio's wife.

After the war, the Bulgaris were venerated with the title of Righteous Among the Nations, an honour bestowed to non-Jews who risked their lives to fight back against the Holocaust. They also received certificates from the British and American armies noting their assistance.

Via Condotti

Via Condotti is the physical and spiritual home of Bulgari. The Roman street is a magnet for upmarket shoppers, thanks to its cluster of prestige luxury brands.

Bulgari's flagship store at 10 Via Condotti first opened in 1905. The new address was an upgrade for the company, but the first iteration of the store – The Old Curiosity Shop – gave no clue as to just how prestigious this address would become.

Between 1932 and 1934, the store closed for a major expansion and refurbishment. The design was led by architects Florestano Di Fausto, Antonio Mina and Eugenio Scanferla. What emerged was an iconic store that would cement some of the stylistic hallmarks of Bulgari that the brand still uses today.

One of the most iconic elements of the new store was its façade. The exterior of the building was clad in cream-coloured travertine limestone, with window arches made from green African marble. This material would become a style signature for Bulgari, and the brand continued its use inside the store with grand marble columns.

Above the doorway to the store, which is in sight of Rome's famous Spanish Steps, was a brand-new sign. In brass letters it spelled out the name of the store, with one small difference. Rather than Bulgari, the new sign read Bvlgari. It was the first time that the branding with the 'v' rather than a 'u' was used.

The lavish store became a magnet for the rich and famous visiting and living in Rome, and was an apt upgrade to reflect the company's new standing as one of the most sought-after jewellers in the world.

In 2014, the famous store would undergo restoration and redesign, led by American architect Peter Marino, to celebrate the brand's 130th anniversary. The fresh design balanced tradition with eclectic style and paid homage to the brand's cultural ties to both Rome and ancient Greece.

OPPOSITE: The Bulgari store on Via dei Condotti, Rome.

BELOW: A view of Rome's Spanish Steps, looking down Via dei Condotti.

Bulgari or Bvlgari?

The new sign above the Via Condotti flagship store may
well have caused some confusion for customers walking past
in 1934. Is the company name still Bulgari, or is it now
Bvlgari? Which is correct? Indeed, the dual spellings still
cause consternation to this day.

For the famous jewellery family, rebranding was nothing new. When Sotirio Voulgaris moved to Italy, he swapped the spelling of his name to Bulgari – a phonetic spelling that would make it easier for his clients to pronounce his Greek name. The change from Bulgari to Bvlgari did the opposite, but it wasn't quite the seismic change that the new shopfront might suggest.

The answer as to whether you should say Bulgari or Bvlgari is simple: Bulgari is the name of the brand and Bvlgari is the logo. The swapping of the 'u' for a 'v' was a stylistic branding move that nodded to the original Voulgaris family name and to Roman numerals. It was a melding of cultures.

Today, you will see the Bvlgari branding across all elements of the jeweller's enterprise, from shopfronts to watch dials and jewellery boxes. But when the name is read or spoken, it is always Bulgari.

OPPOSITE: Marble has become an iconic signature of the brand, as seen in the sign of this Bulgari store in Prague.

Taking Jewels Seriously

When Bulgari first opened what would become its flagship store on Via Condotti, the jewels on display inside – alongside ladles, mirrors and ceramics – were not exactly à la mode. At that time, Italy was culturally and artistically stagnant. While Paris was setting trends and pushing boundaries, Italian jewellery looked pretty much as it had in the 19th century. The Art Nouveau style that was ripping through the rest of Europe never made it south to Italy.

Around 1907, Giorgio Bulgari, who was about 18 at the time, travelled to Paris to buy gems and was amazed by what he found there. He took time to visit local jewellers and in doing so discovered the latest trends, techniques and materials that jewellers such as Cartier were using. He returned home to Italy full of new ideas.

By the 1920s, the focus of Bulgari collections had changed. No longer were the windows overstuffed with antiquated styles catering to tourists. Instead, linear, geometric designs that followed the fashions of Paris were artfully displayed. Art Deco-influenced long sautoirs started to filter through, as did on-trend designs inspired by Asia and Ancient Egypt.

OPPOSITE: This floral Bulgari jewel, with an emerald cabochon at its centre, was part of the 2019 "La Dolce Vita" exhibition at Castel Sant'Angelo, Rome.

ABOVE: A diamond and emerald Bulgari necklace on display at the 2019 "La Dolce Vita" exhibition at Castel Sant'Angelo, Rome.

In the 1930s, the jeweller started to create all-white platinum jewels set with diamonds. The styles were geometric in nature and took inspiration from industrial designs, with nuts-and-bolts motifs and stylised buckles and straps. Platinum was a relatively new precious material at the time, made popular by Cartier's famous Garland-style jewellery. The metal was stronger and more dense than gold,

with a steely sheen. It was perfect for creating complex designs, although working with it required a new skill set.

During this time, the Bulgaris struck up a friendship with a local Roman goldsmith called Ubaldo Crescenzi. It was his dedication to craft that allowed Bulgari to offer these French styles, many of which were technically complex. Crescenzi worked out of an atelier on Via della Fontanella di Borghese, a few minutes' walk from Bulgari's stores. He would later move into the workshop above the brand's Via Condotti store as the relationship strengthened.

During this time, Bulgari also outsourced some of its work to goldsmiths in France. This is why some Bulgari pieces from the 1920s carry French makers' marks and hallmarks alongside the Bulgari signature. It also started to buy in top-quality diamonds and coloured gemstones to set in its designs, which jettisoned its reputation from tourist store to top jeweller. As its reputation spread throughout the city, Bulgari started to attract an even starrier client list.

One of its important early clients was Count Galeazzo Ciano di Cortellazzo, who was Italy's minister of foreign affairs between 1936 and 1943. He was also married to the daughter of Benito Mussolini, the country's reigning dictator. It has been said that between January 1936 and May 1943, the di Cortellazzos spent 300,000 lira – an extortionate amount of money – at Bulgari. A year later, the Count would be dead, executed by the new Italian government put in place after his father-in-law was overthrown.

OPPOSITE: An emerald and diamond Bulgari bracelet previewed by Sotheby's ahead of its 2018 Royal Jewels from the Bourbon Parma Family sale.

Major Stones

A sure-fire way for any jeweller to get noticed is to deal with important stones – not just large, expensive gemstones but historic ones. The Bulgaris realised this, and started to deal in major gemstones in the 1930s.

One of the important stones to pass through Bulgari was a 24.44ct emerald-cut lilac-pink diamond, which was set into a ring. The jeweller sold it to Count Vittorio Cini of Monselice in the 1930s. Count Cini, a rich industrialist and politician, was one of Bulgari's most important clients at that time. He was married to Italian actress Lyda Borelli, who was the recipient of many of his purchases.

Count Cini later sold the lilac-pink diamond ring back to Bulgari, which in turn sold it to another Italian businessman in the 1950s as a gift for his wife. Legend has it that the wife lost the ring in 1970 at a nightclub. It was found at 4am by a cabaret dancer who believed it to be fake, and gave it to his mother as a gift. His mother loved the ring so much that she wished to be buried wearing it, but luckily it was sent for appraisal before this happened, at which point its true value was revealed.

As the ring had never been claimed by its previous owner, the dancer was advised he could sell it at auction. The stone fetched CHF2.97 million at Sotheby's in 1976. It was purchased by jeweller Robert Mouawad, who renamed the stone the Mouawad Lilac.

Another important
gem was the
41.06ct octagonal
Pasha Diamond,
which Bulgari
bought from the
collection of King Farouk of Egypt in the 1940s. It had
originally belonged to Ismail Pasha, the Sultan of Egypt,
after whom it is named. Bulgari sold the enormous diamond
to Barbara Hutton, an American socialite and heiress.
Unfortunately, she found the unusual shape of the diamond
not to her taste and had Cartier recut it to a round shape,
reducing its size to 38.19cts.

A diamond that survived unchanged by a client is the Bulgari
Laguna Blu, an incredibly rare 11.16ct pear-shaped fancy
vivid blue diamond. Bulgari mounted it in a ring and sold
it to a private collector in 1970, and it is believed to be the
most valuable piece ever sold by the brand. In 2023, the
diamond came up for auction at Sotheby's, and to promote
the sale it was worn by Priyanka Chopra at the Met Gala, set
into a necklace. It sold for CHF76 million.

Bulgari's First Signature Design

Every great jewellery house needs a signature design, and for Bulgari its first was the Trombino ring, which was created in 1932. The design was a labour of love for Giorgio

Bulgari, quite literally: it started out as a sketch for a ring with which he hoped to propose to Leonilde Gulienetti. For someone as passionate about jewels as Giorgio, the ring had to be perfect.

His design was for a ring that would elevate the central stone above the band, creating a sense of volume. This prominent setting is what inspired the name Trombino, which translates from Italian as "little trumpet", as the profile does indeed look trumpet-like.

He worked purely in white diamonds, as was the fashion at the time. As well as a central stone, diamonds crowded the band, but rather than simply creating a blanket of stones in a pavé setting, Giorgio sought to add a little flair.

In addition to pavé diamonds, he added graduated baguette-cut diamonds that led away from the central stone, almost like a ladder. This placement of baguettes created an even more prominent stage for that elevated central diamond, drawing the eye to it.

Giorgio was delighted with his final design, and steeled his nerves for the proposal. Leonilde must also have been pleased with it, as she agreed to marry him.

So striking was the ring that it soon caught the attention of Rome society, and Giorgio realised that what had started as a personal project had huge potential for his company. And so, he began to produce the Trombino for his clients, and the 1930s design remains popular to this day.

OPPOSITE: An all-diamond and platinum Bulgari Trombino ring, which sold for US$57,150 at Sotheby's in 2023.

Post-war Creativity

After World War II came to a close, and Italy's fascist dictator Benito Mussolini had fallen from power, the mood of the country was not conducive with high jewellery and expensive gemstones. There was, however, a spirit of looking forward; the Italian people were seeking modernity.

As such, Bulgari needed to change tack, and a concept that felt right for the times was tubogas. This metalsmithing technique was still luxurious – requiring many hours of craftsmanship and much gold – but the result was a sculptural piece of adornment with industrial undertones. It also felt fresh and innovative.

Tubogas was inspired by petrol pumps of the 1920s, hence the name. By wrapping metal strips together rather than using one solid pipe, gas technicians could create a flexible metal tube. Jewellers, including Bulgari, started to experiment with this idea in the 1940s, using precious metals. Two long strips of gold would be wound around a wooden core, which would later be removed. The strips were cut in a way that allowed them to interlock without requiring soldering, creating flexible gold designs.

Bulgari first showed its clients this new technique in 1948, using it to create an early iteration of the Serpenti watch. The timepiece benefitted from the flex in the gold to wrap around the wrist, creating a visually exciting design that was comfortable to wear.

The jeweller used tubogas regularly in the following years, expanding its use to jewellery collections as well as watches. It even created belts made from tubogas.

Sometimes the jeweller would use two strips of the same metal to create an all-yellow gold look; other times it would create a mixed-metal striped look. Tubogas was particularly popular in the 1980s, and while it is used by other jewellers, the technique has become synonymous with Bulgari.

La Dolce Vita

The 1950s marked the beginning of a new hedonistic chapter in Rome's history. The city was brimming with life and glamour, and would soon see an influx of international celebrities as the American and Italian film industries descended on the Eternal City.

This would be an important time for Bulgari. As well as finding itself being called on by the jet set, the Roman jeweller was also fast developing its own signature style. Out went the imitations of Parisian jewels and in came bold, colourful designs that broke the rules of fine jewellery. It was a heady combination that chimed perfectly with the illicit excitement powering the city.

RIGHT: Audrey Hepburn and Gregory Peck in a scene from the 1953 film *Roman Holiday*.

The Theatre of Rome

In the 1950s and 1960s, Rome became just about the most glamorous place on the planet. It was synonymous with fashion, style, glamour, nightlife and sex appeal. The well-heeled jet set descended on the city, using it as a playground and a place to be seen, with paparazzi in hot pursuit.

ABOVE: The original movie poster for the 1960 film *La Dolce Vita*.

OPPOSITE: Actress Anita Ekberg in a scene from *La Dolce Vita*.

It also became an important film location, leading to Rome picking up the nickname 'Hollywood on the Tiber', in reference to the River Tiber that runs through the city. This led to even more international celebrities flocking to Rome.

Roman Holiday, starring Gregory Peck and Audrey Hepburn, became the second-most popular film at the US box office in September 1953. The film was shot almost entirely on location in Rome, and delivered many iconic visuals, such as the actors riding through the streets on a Vespa, Hepburn placing her hand in the Bocca della Verità (Mouth of Truth), and the romantic leads walking down the Spanish Steps, right next to Bulgari's boutique. It was also a pivotal moment for Italian cinema. With all the attention

on Rome and its glamorous lifestyle, local stars such as Gina Lollobrigida and Sophia Loren were jettisoned onto the world stage.

Italian filmmaker Federico Fellini released his masterpiece *La Dolce Vita* in 1960, and the film summed up the glamour and the madness of Rome. The title translates as "the sweet life", and while it was an ironic title for the film, the phrase la dolce vita has been adopted to describe this heady, starry time in Rome's history.

As Martin Scorsese put it, the film went on to "conquer the world". It received three Oscar nominations, among many other awards, and cemented the world's obsession with Rome. An obsession that Bulgari would benefit from.

OPPOSITE TOP: Italian film actress Gina Lollobrigida pictured in Bulgari jewellery in 1968, including a garland of diamond-set flowers that was valued at US$2 million.

OPPOSITE BOTTOM: Ingrid Bergman wearing diamond Bulgari jewellery in the 1964 film *The Visit*.

ABOVE: Sophia Loren and Clark Gable filming the 1960 film *It Started in Naples*.

Star Magnet

The mid-century madness for *La Dolce Vita* was an important turning point for Bulgari. The jeweller had already found success, but the international spotlight that fell on Rome was, in turn, shining on a jeweller that had – since those early abandoned days of international expansion under Sotirio – been very much a local jeweller. Now, Bulgari's shops were making their way on to the must-see list of visiting celebrities, socialites, and those enamoured with the scene.

Bulgari's client list began to read like a red-carpet roster. Grace Kelly, Audrey Hepburn, Jackie Onassis and Anita Ekberg were among the stars known to have travelled to see the famous Roman jeweller on Via Condotti. As the actor Richard Burton joked of his wife Elizabeth Taylor: "The only word in Italian Elizabeth knows is Bulgari."

The A-list appreciation for Bulgari led to its jewels being worn on red carpets, and also in films. Ingrid Bergman wore many pieces by the jeweller in the 1964 film *The Visit*. Sometimes the Bulgari jewels worn on set were actually personal pieces owned by the actresses. This was true of Elizabeth Taylor in 1963's *The V.I.P.s* and Gina Lollobrigida in 1964's *Woman of Straw*.

When Lollobrigida's jewellery collection was put up for auction at Sotheby's in 2013, the majority of the pieces for sale were signed by Bulgari. The top-performing jewels dated back to the 1960s, including a 19.03ct diamond ring that sold for more than $780,000, and a pair of emerald ear clips that sold for more than $306,000. The entire sale fetched nearly $5 million.

The connection between Bulgari and Hollywood has continued and developed since these early days. The jeweller estimates that its creations have been worn in more than 40 productions, and its jewels and watches regularly appear on the red carpet at events such as the Academy Awards, the Golden Globes and the Cannes Film Festival.

ABOVE LEFT: Queen of Iran Soraya Esfandiary-Bakhtiary outside the Bulgari store in Rome in 1964.

ABOVE RIGHT: Sophia Loren in her home in Rome's Palazzo Lovatelli in 1959, wearing Bulgari jewellery.

Elizabeth Taylor

One of Bulgari's most famous clients in its La Dolce Vita era – and long afterwards – was Elizabeth Taylor. The American actor first discovered Bulgari when she was filming *Cleopatra* in 1962. Some of the film was shot on location in Italy, and it is said that when she had time between takes, or wished to escape the paparazzi, she would head to Via Condotti to try on Bulgari's masterpieces. When she did, she was allowed to enter through a secret side door that provided her with a private courtyard in which to park.

Taylor was a famous jewellery collector, and often negotiated pieces of jewellery as part of her film contracts. She even published a book about her obsession in 2002 titled *Elizabeth Taylor: My Love Affair with Jewelry*. Therefore, it was little wonder that downtime in Rome led her to Bulgari.

Taylor's portrayal of Cleopatra also helped to make a Bulgari icon truly stratospheric: the Serpenti watch. Although she didn't wear her watch during filming, she was photographed wearing it on set for a publicity still, and the snake-like design chimed perfectly with the Egyptian theme of the film. Her endorsement of the Serpenti watch transformed a quirky accessory created by a local Roman jeweller into a global icon.

Bulgari wasn't the only burgeoning love affair in Taylor's life at that time. She was also starting a romance with her *Cleopatra* co-star Richard Burton, who would become her

OPPOSITE: Elizabeth Taylor attends a masked ball at Ca' Rezzonico Palace in Venice in 1967, wearing an Alexandre of Paris headdress, and Bulgari jewellery.

BELOW LEFT: Elizabeth Taylor as Cleopatra in the 1963 film of the same name.

BELOW RIGHT: Diamond and sapphire Bulgari jewels owned by Elizabeth Taylor, on display at a Christie's auction preview.

fifth husband in 1964. As such, Burton lavished her with gifts. When speaking about their time together filming in Rome, Burton famously quipped: "I introduced her to beer and she introduced me to Bulgari."

Taylor's own quote to the *New York Times* in 2002 about their jewel-fuelled relationship was just as memorable: "I used to get so excited [when he bought me something], I would jump on top of him and practically make love to him in Bulgari."

What he didn't give her, however, was an engagement ring. Instead, his proposal was accompanied by an emerald and diamond brooch from Bulgari that the actress pinned onto her dress on their first wedding day (the couple would later split and marry for a second time, before splitting again). On their wedding day, he presented her with another piece of Bulgari. It was a lavish collier set with 16 step-cut Colombian emeralds weighing more than 60cts, surrounded by clusters of round, brilliant and pear-shaped diamonds. Taylor later wore this necklace when she picked up her

Oscar for Best Actress in 1966 for her performance in *Who's Afraid of Virginia Woolf?*

Taylor continued to be gifted and collect Bulgari jewellery throughout her life, and amassed an impressive collection. When she died in 2011, her jewellery collection was auctioned off at Christie's a few months later, bringing in a record-breaking $11.8 million. It was the most expensive single-owner collection to be sold at auction.

OPPOSITE: Elizabeth Taylor wearing a Bulgari diamond and emerald Giardinetto brooch at the 1962 David di Donatello Awards.

ABOVE: Elizabeth Taylor on her wedding day in 1964, wearing the Bulgari emerald brooch that Richard Burton proposed with.

Bulgari was among the bidders, buying back nine pieces that are now part of its Bulgari Heritage Collection. It has since hosted exhibitions of the actor's jewels around the world, and has loaned them to celebrities to wear on the red carpet. In 2013, Julianne Moore wore a diamond and emerald Bulgari necklace that had belonged to Taylor, and which the jeweller had acquired at the auction for $6 million.

Other pieces bought back by Bulgari include: an emerald and diamond *en tremblant* (articulated jewels that shimmer with movement) brooch; a gold and turquoise-encrusted 'Cleopatra' mirror made specially for the star; the brooch Burton proposed with; a platinum sautoir with diamonds and sapphires; a Trombino sapphire ring; and a diamond and gold Monete sautoir set with six ancient Roman coins.

The Bulgari Style

The 1960s was a definitive time for Rome, a moment when it came into its own in joyous colour. It was the same for Bulgari. While its initial transition from The Curiosity Shop to fine jeweller had led it to try and follow the fashions of the day, a burgeoning confidence led it to explore its own personality, and develop a signature style that was different to that of the French maisons.

Those early collections had been about luxury, about defining Bulgari as a jeweller of note. To do this, it had looked to Paris and had started working with the finest materials. In the 1930s, Bulgari created all-white designs of platinum and diamonds to fit with the zeitgeist of the day, although every so often it would incorporate a brightly coloured gemstone. This was to be a hint as to where Bulgari was going.

In the 1940s, its aesthetic started to soften. Floral and naturalistic designs began to appear, and gold replaced the cooler platinum. The brand also started to use semi-precious gemstones like citrine in place of diamonds. This use of semi-precious stones was partly due to the mood of the post-war times – these stones were cheaper and less ostentatious – but Bulgari's love affair with these gems ran deeper than fiscal sensitivity. Using them was about fun and self-expression – the embodiment of La Dolce Vita.

OPPOSITE: Carla Bruni models in a Bulgari ad campaign from the 2010s.

ABOVE: A Bulgari
ring set with a
cushion-cut pink
sapphire, accented
with calibré-
cut sapphires
and baguette
diamonds, sold
at Sotheby's for
$19,050 in 2023.

LEFT: Bulgari
necklace set
with rubellites,
amethysts, brilliant-
cut diamonds, pink
tourmaline and
emeralds, sold for
HK$1.1 million at
Sotheby's in 2023.

By the 1960s, the Bulgari style was firmly established. It was one that embraced colour and volume, and prioritised these aesthetics over a jewel's value as a commodity. If turquoise better encapsulated the narrative its designers were trying to deliver than a sapphire, they would use that. Or if a large ruby gave the right scale compared to a better-quality but smaller ruby, volume would win out. It would also sit semi-precious next to precious – something that might have felt sacrilegious to other jewellers.

One of the most important vehicles to deliver the Bulgari style was a gemstone cut called a cabochon. This term refers to a gemstone that has been shaped and polished but not faceted. The effect creates a smooth, domed top with a flat base. The cabcochon cut makes gemstones look fuller and denser, rather than more brilliant – which is the role of facets.

ABOVE: In 2009, to celebrate its 125th anniversary, Bulgari collaborated with Poste Italiane to create a postage stamp featuring one of its necklaces.

OVERLEAF: A turquoise, amethyst and diamond Bulgari necklace on display at its Rodeo Drive store.

ABOVE TOP: A gold, emerald, pearl and diamond Bulgari choker from the collection of Barbara and Frank Sinatra, displayed at a Sotheby's auction preview in 2023.

ABOVE BOTTOM: A suite of colourful sapphire and pearl jewels on display at Bulgari's store on Bond Street, London.

Bulgari was having the cabochons cut and then using them in prominent positions in their designs, perhaps as a central stone for a ring, or spaced evenly on a collier. It would also opt for unusual colour combinations that created a strong sense of playfulness and joy. It is a style that is popular today, but at this time it was entirely innovative and looked different to other major maisons.

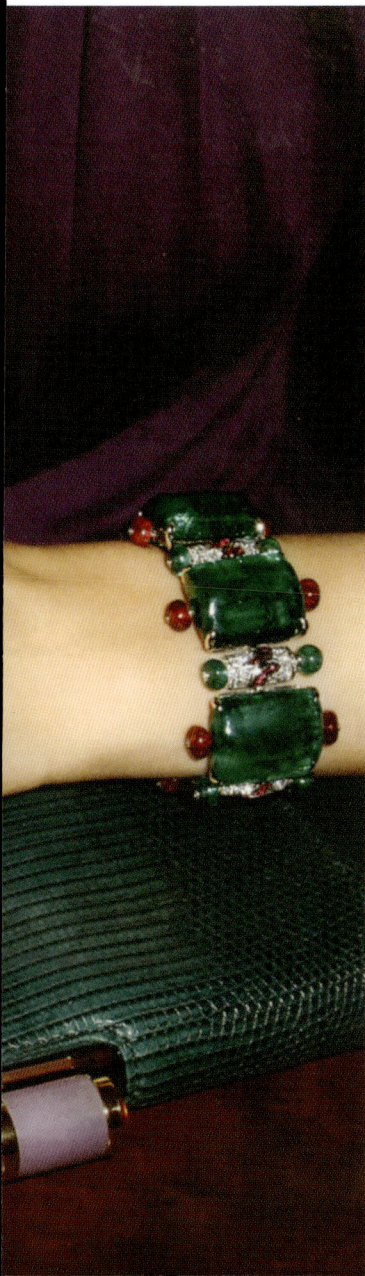

In the 1970s, Bulgari revived another gemstone tradition by using calibré-cut stones to create subtle accents of colour. The calibré technique uses small, custom-cut gemstones in the shape of rectangles, squares, oblongs or other fancy shapes. They are specially cut to fit closely together with no gaps or metal between the stones, giving the impression of an invisible setting.

Bulgari worked with cutters in Germany's famous gem centre in Idar-Oberstein. Calibré cuts are very labour intensive to produce, which is why they had fallen out of fashion in the 1920s.

OPPOSITE: A suite of emerald, as featured in a Bulgari ad campaign.

Designers at Bulgari

The Bulgari design story began with the family driving its creativity. First, Sotirio as founder, then Giorgio taking over as jewellery designer, and many more family members to follow. It has worked with a number of designers from outside the family, too.

One who who had a strong influence on Bulgari in the early days was Gianni Valli. He started working with Bulgari in 1945 and stayed with the brand until a year before his death in 1991. When he first joined, Bulgari was still trying to imitate the maisons of Paris, and Valli was instrumental to its success in doing this. He oversaw the introduction of complex techniques such as *en tremblant* and invisible settings. Valli was also responsible for the awakening of the Bulgari style. He shepherded in the voluptuous settings and bold colour combinations that made it a worldwide name.

In 1976, Bulgari poached American jewellery designer Donald Claflin from Tiffany & Co, which was a major coup, as the talented designer had a stellar reputation. Claflin helped to introduce a smoothness and softer shapes to the collections. One of his designs was a pair of hoop earrings created by a continuous line of baguette-cut diamonds. His style was contemporary and fresh, with predominantly yellow gold jewels that could easily transition from day to night. Sadly, Claflin died just three years after joining Bulgari. He was 44 years old.

OPPOSITE: Jewellery designer Lucia Silvestri photographed wearing a Bulgari necklace.

Many other designers have lent their talent to Bulgari, including the Italian master jeweller Fabio Salini, and Omar Tores, who spent 15 years with the brand. The latest to shape its collections Lucia Silvestri, who became creative director in 2013. Silvestri has built her whole career at Bulgari, starting out in the gemmology department in 1980 at just 18. During her time there, she was mentored closely by Gianni, Paola and Nicola Bulgari. Though she works with a deep respect for the Bulgari style, Lucia has brought her own vision of a more feminine touch to the brand.

Ancient Coins

It was Ubaldo Crescenzi, the goldsmith who moved his practice to the workshop above the Bulgari store on Via Condotti, who is partly responsible for the jeweller's love of ancient coins. As godfather to Nicola Bulgari, the third son of Giorgio, Crescenzi would gift him silver coins from the Roman era on his wedding anniversaries. This sparked an interest in numismatics for Nicola, and it would lead to one of Bulgari's most famous collections – Monete.

The Monete collection features jewels set with ancient coins rather than gemstones. One of the earliest examples is a necklace from 1966 with two solid gold coins, one depicting Roman emperor Justinian I, who was in power between 527 and 565, and the other of emperor Leo I, who ruled between 457 and 474.

This technique was in no way invented by Bulgari. Jewellers have set coins into items of adornment for centuries. Indeed, Sotirio set faux coins into silver jewellery in the late 19th century. But it is a technique that the brand has become famous for.

Monete pieces, sometimes referred to as Gemme Nummarie, predominantly use Ancient Roman and Ancient Greek coins – a nod to both parts of the brand's heritage – but on occasion it has used more contemporary coins. In 1976, for example, it made jewels set with early American one-dollar coins to mark the bicentennial of the American revolution. "The history of coins is the history of mankind," Nicola Bulgari told *Architectural Digest* in 2009. "If you study the coinage of a while civilization, it's extraordinary what you find out about the way people lived and thought then."

A New Generation

Giorgio and Constantino Bulgari both had children who would follow them into the family business, each making their own contribution to the Italian jeweller's legacy.

Constantino was the first to have children, with his wife Laura giving birth to two daughters. Anna Bulgari was born in 1927 and Marina Bulgari in 1930. Both would be involved in the design of Bulgari's jewels and the running of the company.

Anna worked in the design department until 1984 and stayed on as a silver consultant until 1990. In 1987, she followed in the footsteps of her author father and published her own book, *Maestri Argentieri, Gemmari e Orafi di Roma* (Master Silversmiths, Gemmologists and Goldsmiths of Rome).

Marina started off in the office of Bulgari, doing administrative tasks but later joined the design team. When Giorgio died in 1966, she would assume control with her cousin Gianni Bulgari as joint chief executives. Marina worked for Bulgari until 1976, and two years later launched her own successful jewellery brand, Marina B.

Giorgio had four children: Lia Bulgari was born in 1933, Giovanni 'Gianni' Bulgari in 1935, Paolo Bulgari in 1937, and Nicola Bulgari in 1941. Giorgio had taken over the day-to-day running of the business in 1945 to allow Constantino to focus on his academic studies. When Giorgio died in 1966, it was to the five cousins – Marina, Anna, Gianni, Paolo and Nicola – that the business would pass. Constantino died in 1973.

It was the three brothers who took on central roles at Bulgari. Gianni, the eldest, designed collections and was involved in buying gemstones. He was also one of Rome's most eligible bachelors in the 1960s, thanks to his good looks and glamorous job. He was described as a playboy in

OPPOSITE: Gianni Bulgari, Nicola Bulgari and Anna Bulgari, photographed together in 1974.

ABOVE: Paolo Bulgari photographed leaving his home in Rome in 1975.

the international press and was often seen in the company of glamorous women, including famous actresses.

Gianni studied for a philosophy and law degree before joining the family business in the early 1960s. When his father died, Gianni led the business with his cousin Marina as joint chief executives. In the 1970s, Gianni had added art director to his job titles and led an overhaul of the business, including launching its watch division. In 1987, after falling out with his brothers, he sold his stake in the firm.

Paolo joined the family business at the age of 18. He was a law student at the time, but had been asked by his father to help design Bulgari's jewellery collections. This would lead to him creating some of the company's most high-profile designs. In 1984, Paolo became chairman of Bulgari.

Nicola had a reputation as a born salesman, and after joining the family business in the 1960s, he split his time between Rome and New York, meeting with important clients. He was also responsible for the launch of Bulgari's perfume business in the US.

Nicola ended up moving to New York in the 1980s, where he made some influential friends, including the artist Andy Warhol. The pair interviewed each other for Warhol's magazine *Interview*. In the article, Warhol said: "I think your jewellery is the 80s... everybody is trying to copy this look." To which Nicola replied: "But they can't because we are always breaking our heads to do better, always better."

Warhol was a fan of the brand as well as the man. He owned many pieces of Bulgari jewellery, and famously once said: "When I am in Rome, I always visit Bulgari, because it is the most important museum of contemporary art."

Another family member who proved instrumental to the Bulgari story was Francesco Trapani, the son of Giorgio's daughter Lia, who was born in 1957. Trapani took over the running of Bulgari in 1984, and is credited with supercharging its commercial success and making it a global brand. He was also instrumental in the sale of Bulgari to LVMH in 2011.

ABOVE: Francesco Trapani photographed holding a Bulgari necklace in 2005.

The Kidnap of Gianni Bulgari

In the 1970s, many of the well-heeled citizens of Rome had started to travel with handguns or bodyguards due to a spate of mafia-led kidnappings. Gianni Bulgari refused to do so, describing such a protected existence as not how he wished to live. Perhaps if he had, what happened on 14th March, 1975, might not have taken place. Gianni was ambushed and snatched while travelling through the city in a limousine. The kidnappers held him for ransom.

The story garnered huge international interest. Gianni was an incredibly glamorous member of the jet set, who had been linked to many famous women. He was tall, blonde and incredibly good looking, with some seriously glitzy pastimes that included flying his own planes, skin diving and racing sportscars competitively. He was a poster boy for the 1960s Italian dream.

The story garnered much publicity throughout the time he was held. It also impacted Rome's luxury scene, with all

stores on Via Condotti closing their doors the day after the kidnapping as a sign of solidarity.

Gianni was held captive in a box for 30 days. During this time, the kidnappers negotiated an astronomical ransom with his brothers Paolo and Nicola. Eventually, an agreement was reached. The Bulgaris paid $2 million for Gianni's release. He was returned on 14th April, and photographs from that day show him looking gaunt and bearded.

Gianni was not the only Bulgari to be kidnapped. In 1983, his cousin Anna Bulgari was kidnapped, along with her teenage son Giorgio after three armed men broke into their home in Rome. The kidnappers demanded 3 billion lira. When the Bulgaris refused to pay, the men cut off Giorgio's ear and increased the ransom to 4 billion lira, which the family paid. Anna and Giorgio were held captive for 36 days.

OPPOSITE: Gianni Bulgari, who had a reputation as a playboy, photographed in 1972.

LEFT: Gianni Bulgari shakes hands with a well-wisher in Rome, just hours after his kidnappers released him on 14th April, 1975.

Watches

B ulgari might be best known for its show-stopping jewels, but the Italian jeweller is also a skilled horologist. Its journey to becoming a provocative watchmaker started almost by accident, when the gift of a digital watch to its best clients sparked a demand it couldn't ignore.

It would spend the next few decades establishing a presence in Switzerland, home of watchmaking, building its horological prowess through key acquisitions. The result is a thriving watch business that creates must-have branded designs, bold high jewellery watches, and a series of watches that consistently smashes world records.

LEFT: Watches on display at a Bulgari store in Milan.

A History of Bulgari Watches

It is likely that S. Bulgari started trading in watches as soon as it opened its doors, but the first known examples of Bulgari watches date back to the 1920s. At that time, Bulgari was trying to align itself with the French jewellery houses and so adopted the Art Deco stylings of the time to produce dainty, yet elaborate, diamond and platinum dress watches for women. Bulgari also produced men's watches. One design from the 1930s has Greek meander motifs on the dial, in a nod to the family's origins.

It was another Hellenic motif that would strengthen Bulgari's reputation for watches in the 1940s: the snake. It started to create watches that looked like snakes around this time, and they soon matured into the Serpenti line, which remains a worldwide success to this day. The watches took advantage of the jeweller's work with tubogas to create a coiling, flexible gold strap.

While the Serpenti became iconic, thanks in part to stars such as Elizabeth Taylor wearing it, it wasn't until the 1970s that Bulgari started to really take watches seriously. And it started almost by happenstance.

Fresh from his kidnapping, with a new sense of urgency and focus, Gianni Bulgari came up with the idea of creating an unusual gift for clients. It was a digital watch in a gold case, engraved with the words Bvlgari Roma. The strap was woven hemp, inspired by macramé bags.

OPPOSITE: A Bulgari Octo chronograph.

RIGHT: Lorenzo Viotti, chief conductor-designate of the Netherlands Philharmonic Orchestra, stars in a campaign for Bulgari watches.

BELOW: An Octo Roma Chronograph watch with mechanical manufacture movement.

The gift, given only to its top 100 clients for Christmas in 1975, proved to be a hit, and requests for more models was such that Bulgari started to make a commercial line of watches based on the design. It was called Bvlgari Bvlgari, and launched in 1977.

It was a sage move. Early sales were good, and in response they set up a dedicated watch division in 1980. Two years later, a brand new company called Bulgari Time was created in the Swiss watch heartland Neuchâtel. This was the company's first step towards making its own watches from start to finish.

Over the next two decades, Bulgari designed and launched more models. Some were sporty twists on Bvlgari Bvlgari; others embraced its reputation as a jeweller, such as the increasingly stylish Serpenti lines, and the collection of Parentesi watches that launched in 1985.

At this point in its watchmaking history, Bulgari was still relying on more mature watchmakers to supply movements. It used calibres from manufacturers including Audemars Piguet, Vacheron Constantin, Jaeger-LeCoultre and Movado.

In 1989, it entered into a partnership with Girard-Perregaux to handle all technical aspects of its watches. This led to its watches becoming more technical. In 1994, it launched its Scuba line of watches that were COSC certified and waterproof to 200m. Also that year, it launched a line of Grandes Complications that offered technically advanced features such as tourbillons and minute repeaters. These watches were made to order for clients, so they were limited in number.

Bulgari's growth as global brand benefitted its watch division. By 1995, it had 36 stores around the world and a further 120 points of sale for its watches.

Innovation was a key focus for the development team. In 1993, as a nod to the original watch's unusual mix of materials, Bulgari released a limited-edition Bvlgari Bvlgari watch made of gold and black plastic. This idea would be expanded on in 2005 with the launch of a Bvlgari Bvlgari chronograph called Carbongold that swapped out the plastic for carbon fibre.

ABOVE: A 2017 ad campaign for Serpenti watches, as seen at Zürich airport in Switzerland.

In 2000, Bulgari Time made a bold move. It bought two other companies – Gérald Genta and Daniel Roth, both of which were leaders in high watchmaking. The companies had previously been bought by Asian retail group The Hour Glass, from which Bulgari acquired them. A new company called Daniel Roth et Gérald Genta Haute Horlogerie was created and based in Le Sentier, Switzerland.

More acquisitions of Swiss companies followed. In 2005, it bought a 50 per cent stake in watch dial specialist Cadrans Designs and a 51 per cent stake in bracelet maker d'Or Prestige, and then in 2007 it bought case specialist Finger. All of these acquisitions were designed to strengthen its manufacturing capabilities, and set it up as a serious horological player.

Record-breaking Watches

As Bulgari set about embedding itself in the watch industry through acquisitions, the skill set it now commanded was vast, and it tapped into this to show the world just how much of a haute horlogerie contender it was.

In 2012, Bulgari relaunched the Octo watch. The octagonal case timepiece was first designed and released by legendary watchmaker Gérald Genta, under his own name. It shared a style similar to another of Genta's masterpieces, the Audemars Piguet Royal Oak. Genta's other design credits include Patek Philippe's Nautilus, IWC's Ingenieur and Omega's Constellation. He was also called on by numerous other brands including Van Cleef & Arpels, Cartier, Chaumet and Seiko, to name a few.

A decision was made to use the Octo line as a showcase for Bulgari's horological prowess, and in 2014 it unveiled the Octo Finissimo Tourbillon. This twist on the Octo was of note due to its thinness: the case measured just 5mm, setting a world record. The same watch picked up a second record for the thinnest tourbillon movement, which was just 1.95mm thick. The watch caused quite the stir in the global watch community and cast Bulgari in a new light – no longer just a jeweller making watches, but a serious player on the Swiss Made scene.

Bulgari followed up in 2016 with the Octo Finissimo Minute Repeater. At 6.85mm, it was thicker than the Octo Finissimo Tourbillon, but the complex nature of the minute

OPPOSITE: An Octo Finissimo automatic watch on display during the 2019 Baselworld fair in Basel, Switzerland.

movement made it another record breaker. The ultra-thin minute repeater movement – housed in a titanium case to amplify the sound of the chiming mechanism that is the hallmark of this complication – was 3.12mm thick.

The following year, Bulgari presented another ultra-thin watch. The Octo Finissimo Automatic was not complex in terms of watchmaking, but it set a new record for size as the thinnest automatic watch on the market at 5.15mm, with a movement just 2.23mm tall.

Bulgari's next attempt would break two records. In 2018, it presented the Octo Finissimo Tourbillon Automatic. It was the thinnest automatic watch at 3.95mm, and also the thinnest tourbillon in the world.

The obsession with record-breaking ultra-thin watchmaking rolled on. In 2019, the Octo Finissimo Chronograph GMT became the thinnest mechanical chronograph movement at 3.3mm, set in a 6.9mm titanium case. In 2020, the Octo Finissimo Tourbillon Chronograph Skeleton Automatic was named the thinnest tourbillon chronograph with a case depth of 3.5mm. And in 2021, the Octo Finissimo Perpetual Calendar became the thinnest perpetual calendar watch at 5mm thick.

In 2022, to mark the 10-year anniversary of the relaunch of the Octo line, Bulgari presented another impressive watch that smashed the others out of the park. The Octo Finissimo Ultra became the thinnest mechanical watch on the planet, with a case size of just 1.8mm.

OPPOSITE: Automatic tourbillon from Bulgari's Octo Finissimo collection.

BELOW LEFT: Bulgari Octo Finissimo Skeleton 8 Days (on left) on display next to an Armin Strom timepiece at an exhibition of Fondation du Grand Prix d'Horlogerie de Genève (GPHG) 2022 award nominees.

BELOW RIGHT: A black ceramic Bulgari Octo Finissimo.

Serpenti Style

The snake-like Serpenti was Bulgari's first icon of watchmaking, and continues to be one of its most famous – and original – designs. The first Serpenti watch was released in 1948, with a supple tubogas coil acting as the serpentine body of the creature and wraparound strap. This was a watch women could easily put on without any assistance. It was a bold, empowering style statement for those brave enough to wear it.

By the 1950s and 1960s, Serpenti watches started to take on a new look. In addition to the more abstract tubogas designs Bulgari had already been producing, it introduced more lifelike designs with realistic-looking heads set with diamond eyes. Attention was paid to the body of the snake, with the introduction of gold scales, often decorated with diamonds, coloured gemstones or swathes of bright enamel. This was no longer the suggestion of a snake, but a seemingly live, writhing serpent coiling around the arm.

The watch dials were hidden within the snakes' hinged heads; to tell the time, the mouth of the snake had to be prized open. Some of these early models had forked tongues. To power these jewellery watches, Bulgari teamed with the leading movement manufacturers of the day, Jaeger-LeCoultre, Vacheron Constantin and Piaget. Some of these early models were co-signed by Bulgari and the movement maker; this ended in the 1970s when Bulgari started producing its own movements.

OPPOSITE: Serpenti Tubogas Infiniti watch in 18-carat rose gold set with diamonds and a full diamond pavé dial.

Snakes were very much in fashion at that time. As *Vogue* editor Diana Vreeland, who owned a Bulgari Serpenti necklace, told her staff in a 1968 memo: "[The serpent] should be on every finger and all wrists... we cannot see enough of them."

The 1970s led to the revival of the tubogas style of Serpenti, reflecting an increasingly casual sartorial mood. During this decade, Bulgari stopped making the scaled designs, although revived them in 2021 as part of its high jewellery offer.

It was also in the 1970s that Bulgari introduced two-tone Serpenti watches, using gold and steel strips to create the wrapped design. Due to production complexities relating to the metals' differing melting points, those

early bi-metal models cost more than the pure gold versions.

The Serpenti has continued to shapeshift over the years. In the 1980s, the tubogas wrap strap was introduced to the Bvlgari Bvlgari collection, and then in 2009, to mark the brand's 125th anniversary, a geometric line of watches with angular heads and scales arrived. In 2016, Serpenti Incanti was a new twist on the motif, with a cross-over design, while 2017's Serpenti Twist offered a more casual and accessible version that replaced a gold bracelet with wraparound leather straps in bold colours.

Snakes are symbols of rebirth and renewal, and it is likely that Bulgari will never stop reinventing the much-loved Serpenti.

OPPOSITE: Fashion editor Anna Dello Russo wearing a Serpenti watch during Milan Fashion Week, 2021.

LEFT: A guest poses with a gemstone-encrusted Serpenti during a benefit for the Pacific Symphony at the Bulgari boutique in Costa Mesa, California.

The Icons

Bulgari has created an armoury of iconic designs that span both jewellery and watches, and each collection tells us something about the evolution of the brand. Which will be your favourite: the coils of Serpenti, the colourful blooms of Giardinetto, or Monete with its use of real ancient coins? Or perhaps you favour the sleek branding of the Bvlgari Bvlgari watches, or the bold silhouette of the Octo timepieces.

Dive into the origin stories of Bulgari's greatest hits, learn how to identify them, and discover which famous faces also own them. Plus, discover the techniques required to make each of these pieces, and what makes them so special.

RIGHT: Charlize Theron wearing a Serpenti necklace and Bulgari diamond necklace at the 2019 *Vanity Fair* Oscars party.

Trombino

The Trombino, which translates from Italian as "little trumpet", is Bulgari's iconic cocktail ring. The design was created by Giorgio Bulgari in 1932, and was instantly eye catching as the central gem stood proud above a bold ring profile studded with diamonds. True to the Bulgari style, the Trombino plays with scale to create a dramatic effect; this is a bold ring that wants to be seen.

While often worn as a right-hand ring, the Trombino can also be worn as an engagement ring. Indeed, the first-ever Trombino was created to be exactly that. That first Trombino ring, which Giorgio designed for his wife to be, was set entirely with diamonds, but later iterations often use coloured gemstones to deliver that classic Bulgari style.

The style of Trombino rings can vary. The first choice is the central gemstone, which can be nearly any shape or size: step-cut, cabochon, oval cut, baguette cut, round... For the diamond – or, indeed, gem-set – shoulders, some rings have strips of gold delineating between the different cuts of diamonds, while others minimise the visible metal to make it appear as though the ring is seamlessly blanketed in stones.

Trombino rings regularly show up at auction. One of the most famous examples is one that belonged to Elizabeth Taylor. The actor, and ferocious Bulgari collector, bought the 1930s ring in 1970 to complement a Bulgari sapphire and diamond sautoir she owned. The ring has a higher-

RIGHT: A sapphire and diamond Trombino ring, which sold at Sotheby's for CHF226,800 in 2022.

than-normal profile, even for Trombino, as it is set with a
magnificent 25ct deep-blue sapphire in a sugarloaf cabochon
cut. Graduated baguette-cut diamonds are set either side
of the sapphire, and the ring is blanketed with round
diamonds. It sold at Christie's in 2011 for $866,500.

ABOVE: An 18-carat gold Serpenti Tubogas watch
with diamonds and a silver opaline dial.

Tubogas

Tubogas refers to a type of metalsmithing that is used across many Bulgari jewellery and watch collections. It is characterised by flexible lengths of gold that appear to be sectioned into smaller horizontal strips.

This simple pattern hides a complex secret. Tubogas, which Bulgari first introduced in the 1940s, is made by wrapping long gold strips with raised edges around a copper or wood core. The gold strips interlock as they are wound, and so don't require soldering. Often, Bulgari will mix metals to create a striped effect. Once the core is removed, what is left is a stretchy, flexible length of gold that can be easily coiled around a wrist or neck.

The most famous use of tubogas is in Bulgari's Serpenti watch collection. This flexible way of working with gold has allowed the brand to create long straps that can wind up the arm – wrapping around as many as six times. They require no clasps to hold them in place.

Tubogas also appears in some of Bulgari's jewellery collections. Sometimes it is simply a decorative nod to the house's brand identity; other times it has a function, such as making jewels like cuffs and necklaces easy to put on.

In 2023, Bulgari introduced a new innovation in tubogas with Serpenti Infiniti. For the first time, the brand was able to set diamonds into the stretchy gold straps. However, to do so its craftspeople had to move away from using long, continuous strips of metal. Instead, it created individual gold rings that could be set with diamonds. These are then assembled on to a flexible titanium blade.

Serpenti

Serpenti is, without doubt, Bulgari's most iconic design of all time. The design takes its inspiration from snakes, with jewel-studded serpentine heads and winding tails.

The first Serpenti, designed in 1948, was a bracelet watch, but the motif has spread far and wide throughout Bulgari's watch and jewellery collections. Some designs make use of the signature tubogas flexible gold to create sinuous tails, while others use articulated gold scales to bring in a more geometric flexibility to bracelets and necklaces.

How snake-like the Serpenti designs are also varies collection to collection. Some are realistic, with glossy enamel or hardstone scales, gems for eyes and heads that open to reveal secret watch faces. Then there are the more abstract designs that offer a far more simplified serpent silhouette.

The Serpenti Seduttori lines are inspired by the scales of a snake only. The sleek scales knit together to form watch bracelets, or cluster to create chandelier earrings.

The Serpenti jewellery collection ranges from minimal

everyday bracelets to fully diamond-set high jewellery necklaces that wrap around the neck. These masterpieces are often seen on the red carpet, worn by celebrities such as Zendaya, Bella Hadid, Naomi Watts and Jennifer Lopez.

Sometimes stars will flip the necklace, wearing it with the snake's head inching down their spines to show off an open-backed dress. Men have also been spotted in shorter versions of the Serpenti necklace, using it to bring an edge to T-shirts worn under suits, or to peek out from beneath a shirt collar in place of a tie.

This enduring Bulgari motif has also been worked into its handbag offering. The Serpenti line of bags have slithering golden snake handles, or enamelled snake head clasps.

OPPOSITE: A gold, diamond and mother-of-pearl Serpenti, spotted during Milan Fashion Week, 2019.

RIGHT: A Serpenti ring and necklace in white gold and diamonds.

Giardinetto

The Giardinetto brooches emerged from the Bulgari workshops for the first time in the early 1960s. The designs take the form of bunches of flowers and fruit, positioned within a vase or basket, set with colourful assortments of cabochon and calibré-cut gemstones.

The brooches were inspired by traditional Italian floral jewels of the same name. Giardinetto translates into English as "little garden" and the term has been used to describe such jewels since the 17th century. Many of the other major jewellery houses, including Cartier, have created similar homages to the style.

The designers at Bulgari chose brightly hued stones to bring their Giardinetto brooches to life. How valuable those stones were was less important than the impact they could bring to a design, so often they chose to use semi-precious gems rather than emeralds, sapphires and rubies.

The Giardinetto brooches' interpretation of nature can be literal, with diamond-set stems tipped with ruby flowers or Indian-style gems carved into petals or leaves. The brooches can also be more abstract cornucopias of turquoise beads, precious cabochons and emerald leaves. Some brooches were made with matching earrings.

A hallmark of some of the finer Giardinetto brooches is the inclusion of the setting technique called *en tremblant*. It is a French term that means 'to tremble' and it refers to the use of tiny hidden springs that make sections of a jewel gently shake, causing diamonds to emit even more sparkle.

Bulgari Giardinetto brooches are highly sought after at
auction, and good examples can fetch tens of thousands of
pounds.

Monete

Monete is Bulgari's homage to ancient coins. The first of these jewels launched in 1966 and while adding coins to jewellery was not a new concept – the Ancient Romans had been doing it long before the Bulgaris did – it is an aesthetic that the brand has come to own.

Rather than recreate the look of coins, each piece within the Monete collections uses real coins that were once in circulation in Ancient Greece or Ancient Rome. Each piece is a one-off – a rare chance to wear a historical artefact. The coins, which can be 2,000 years old, are made in silver, gold or bronze, and will depict important historical figures from the past.

Antique coins have been incorporated into all types of Bulgari jewellery, from simple pendants and cufflinks to large tubogas chokers and signet rings. A recuring theme within the Monete collection is its use of heavy gold curb-link chain, which is perhaps a hangover from the collection's heyday in the 1980s.

The coins are left untouched, preserved simply in their gold settings, which follow the often-irregular contours, so as not to diminish their value. The designs around them, however, can be elaborate. One set, which sold at Christie's in 2023 for £217,000, included a necklace that had an Ancient Roman bronze coin set at the centre of a pink opal and diamond pendant.

In 2023, actress and Bulgari ambassador Anne Hathaway

brought fresh attention to the Monete collection when she wore a bold choker and bracelet to the Met Gala. The sculptural yellow gold choker, which was fully diamond set, featured at its centre a single silver coin that dated back to 400–350 B.C. The bracelet had a coin from the ancient kingdom of Macedonia dating to 336–323 B.C.

ABOVE: A gold and diamond Monete necklace set with an ancient Greek coin, which once belonged to Mary Tyler Moore, on display at an auction preview at Sotheby's New York.

Bvlgari Bvlgari

The Bvlgari Bvlgari watch is one of the Italian brand's most iconic products, but it was never meant to be for sale. The first of these watches was originally made as a Christmas gift for its best 100 clients in 1975.

That first iteration was a digital watch with a gold case. On the bezel, the brand engraved "Bvlgari Roma". It was presented on a plated hemp and leather strap. Bulgari's clients loved it. Requests started to flood in for more of the unusual timepieces, with collector interest no doubt stoked by the limited and exclusive nature of the line.

What really landed with clients was the bold Bvlgari Roma branding on the bezel, and this has become the cornerstone of the Bvlgari Bvlgari collection. The first collection launched in 1977. The digital display and quirky strap were replaced with a sleek minimalist dial and leather strap, but the bold branding remained.

By 1980, Bulgari started to add its brand name to the dial of the watches – this can be a handy tool for dating the earliest of these timepieces. It was also in this year that Bulgari added a Bvlgari Bvlgari watch face to a Serpenti tubogas strap.

There have been many iterations of the line since then, including aesthetic flourishes, such as diamond details and hardstone dials, and horological extras such as chronograph, tourbillon, moonphase and retrograde complications, as well as skeletonised versions. What always remains is that iconic bezel.

ABOVE: A pair of Bvlgari Bvlgari watches
on display in a store in Milan.

Parentesi

In 1982, Bulgari launched an innovative new collection of jewellery called Parentesi that was designed to be modular. The first collection was made using three elements: one shaped like an hourglass, a second with a curved section, and a third T-shaped element. By removing some of these elements, the sizing or function of pieces could quickly be changed.

Parentesi was the brainchild of Gianni Bulgari, who was doodling during a design meeting when he came up with the idea. He had been sketching brackets when he was struck by the potential of composable elements for jewellery.

The interlocking element was inspired by the paving stones of Rome. It was also driven by a desire to create jewels that could give flexibility and be worn in many ways. For example, by removing some links a necklace could become a bracelet. It also meant that clients could build on their collections, adding more components as time and budget allowed, giving their collections ever greater potential.

Parentesi was also a vehicle to help Bulgari reach a wider audience. By mixing gold and steel components, the price of these jewels was much more accessible than Bulgari's solid gold jewellery. The production methods used also kept prices lower, as the factories could produce lots of these simple elements in bulk. They would then be assembled by craftspeople to create any number of designs.

Parentesi is one of Bulgari's boldest looks, and an iconic silhouette that has been much copied. You will find it across rings, chokers, watches, bracelets, and more. Some designs also include components that have been set with diamonds to bring a flash of luxury to these versatile pieces.

OPPOSITE: A gold and diamond Parentesi collier and ear clips, which sold as a set for €40,640 at Sotheby's in 2023.

B.zero1

Bulgari often takes inspiration from Roman architecture, and the profile of the B.zero1 ring was designed as an homage to the Colosseum. The tall, stacked profile of the ring matches the circular stories of the famous arena.

The unusual name of this collection relates to when it was launched. The "B", of course, stands for Bulgari, while the "zero" relates to the new millennium, and the "1" represents new beginnings.

The gold B.zero1 designs are characterised by two solid rings, stamped with the Bvlgari Bvlgari logo. The section between these two rings calls for the house's tubogas skills, with bands of metal wound around the centre.

The industrial spool-like design is incredibly versatile. It plays with scale by adjusting the number of bands in the centre (between one and five), and also plays with colour by introducing yellow, rose or white gold. The central section can also be adorned with diamonds or inlaid with enamel.

Bulgari has also used this collection as a vehicle for collaboration, inviting creatives including British-Indian sculptor Anish Kapoor and late Iraqi-British architect Zaha Hadid to create their own versions.

B.zero1 was first launched in 1999, and since then it has become Bulgari's most commercially successful line by volume, with more than 2 million rings sold worldwide. The B.zero1 motif is now applied to many types of jewellery, including rings, earrings, necklaces and bracelets. In 2020, Bulgari introduced a new look with the B.zero1 Rock line, which has studded spirals at its centre.

Since the B.zero1 ring is so iconic, it has led to many copycats. To avoid purchasing a fake ring, look for the individual serial number that is engraved on each genuine Bulgari B.zero1 ring and call a store to ask them to match the records.

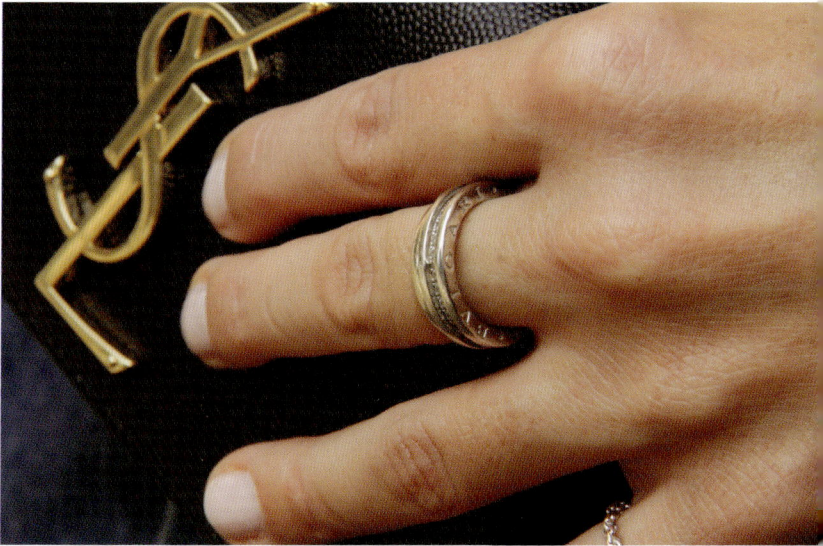

ABOVE: A gold and diamond B.zero1 ring, spotted during Milan Fashion Week, 2015.

RIGHT: A gold B.zero1 ring.

Octo

The Bulgari Octo is a cult timepiece, but it didn't always belong to Bulgari. The timepiece was actually designed by legendary watchmaker Gérald Genta in the 1980s and released under his name. In 1996, Genta sold his business to Asian watch retailer The Hour Glass, from which Bulgari bought the Gerald Genta business, including the rights to the Octo.

The Octo has a similar DNA to the Audemars Piguet Royal Oak, another of Genta's designs, and is so named for its octagonal case shape, which has at its centre a round bezel. Bulgari launched its first version of the Octo in 2012, and in doing so marked itself out as a serious watch player.

The first Octo was made available in steel or rose gold. It had a black lacquer dial of intense colour, which was achieved by applying a dozen coats of lacquer via a unique process developed in-house.

Since then, Bulgari has experimented with material and colour combinations. Octo models range from classic blue dials on full metal bracelets, to skeletonised models, and even jewellery watches. In 2023, Bulgari released a model with a bracelet and case made from carbon.

As well as offering up fresh aesthetics, Bulgari also used the Octo as a vehicle for innovation. In 2014, the Octo Finissimo (Italian for 'very fine') was launched with the aim to make a very thin watch. The first was 5.15mm thick, and this was just the opening gambit. The race for thinness has continued, and the brand has set multiple records in the process. In 2022, it released the Octo Finissimo Ultra, a titanium watch that measured just 1.8mm.

PREVIOUS: A steel Octo Finissimo
with small seconds sub dial, on
display at a store in Japan.

BELOW: An 18-carat rose gold
Lvcea watch with diamonds and
a synthetic pink sapphire crown.

Lvcea

Bulgari launched Lvcea as a ladies' dress watch in 2014. Its
design notes claim the watch to be inspired by sundials –
the timekeeper of choice in Ancient Rome.

Tying in with the sun theme, the watches often have a

luminosity to them. This could be achieved by adding diamonds, mother-of-pearl dials, or sunburst dials (an engraving technique).

In 2021, Bulgari released the Lvcea Intarsio Marquetry watch, which has a mother-of-pearl marquetry dial that creates a beautiful play of light by alternating between light-grey and dark-grey slices of the lustrous material. It followed this up in 2024 with a bold green malachite marquetry dial.

The signature element of this watch design is the crown. Each one is set with a coloured gemstone – often a cabochon-cut synthetic rubellite or synthetic sapphire that is tipped with a diamond.

The round dials are kept simple, with Bvlgari branding and minimalist hands. Most models have diamonds marking the hours, with the option of a date window. Some Lvcea timepieces with more unusual dials forgo the hour markers altogether. This is true of those with dials made of aventurine, a gold-flecked blue crystal said to be a psychic activator, and its skeletonised models, which show tumbling letters over the movement that spell out Bvlgari.

The watches are powered by either an automatic movement, or a battery-powered quartz movement. And there are a number of bracelet options within Lvcea. The most classic is the stacked metal bracelet, which was inspired by Bulgari's Serpenti line. It is also offered with colourful alligator leather straps, and in 2018 the brand released a line of Lvcea watches with tubogas bracelets.

BELOW: An 18-carat rose gold Diva's Dream watch set with brilliant-cut diamonds, pink tourmalines and turquoise.

Diva's Dream

On the floors of the historic Baths of Caracallain in Rome are fan-shaped tiles that have remained intact for thousands of years. These well-worn artefacts were the inspiration for Bulgari's Diva's Dream collection, which launched in 2016.

The collection is the brainchild of designer Lucia Silvestri, and is characterised by elegant fan shapes that mimic the shape of the tiles. She designed it for the modern woman, and the name reflects this. The collection is a celebration of feminine power, and Bulgari encourages its clients to embrace their inner divas when wearing it.

At its simplest, a Diva's Dream jewel might be a single gold fan, set with diamonds or inlaid with hardstone like malachite or carnelian, and set on a chain as a necklace or bracelet. The shape has also appeared in high jewellery and watch collections, and is instantly recognisable as a Bulgari signature design.

There is also a Diva's Dream watch collection in which the motif is interpreted in a number of ways. Sometimes the fan shape hangs from the case as a charm; other times it makes up a repeating pattern on the dial or loops the watch face to form an elaborate bezel. Other nods to the famous shape include fan-shaped lugs that connect the case to the strap, and a metal strap that is made up of tiled gold fans.

The versatility and sensuous shapes of this collection is what makes it a mainstay for collectors. And with an instantly recognisable signature, it is also a collection that performs well on the secondary market.

Fiorever

Bulgari has been designing floral jewellery for more than a century, but in 2018 it began a new chapter with the launch of the Fiorever jewellery collection. The contemporary collection is a linear interpretation of the flower – a sharp contrast to the naturalistic blooms of its Giardinetto brooches.

The Fiorever central motif is four petals with a central gemstone pistil. The petals are split into two parts, with a smaller gold section separated by a slice of negative space to create a more complex twist on a simple quatrefoil shape.

Fiorever jewels are crafted in yellow, rose and white gold, set with diamonds and coloured gemstones. Pieces within the collection range from simple studs and pendants to glamorous colliers and bracelets that would work well for evening glamour.

Indeed, many stars have worn the Fiorever jewels on the red carpet, including Selena Gomez, who wore white gold and diamond rings from the collection to the Golden Globes in 2024. It has also been modelled by Bulgari ambassadors Úrsula Corberó – who was the original face of the line when it first launched – and Anne Hathaway in various promotional shots.

Fiorever's floral interpretation is said to be inspired by a classic Roman motif. According to Bulgari, the four-leaf flower is a symbol of Italians' passion for life. The symbol, it says, can be found decorating many ancient builds, including the garden frescoes of Villa di Livia and the ceiling mosaics of the Santa Costanza Mausoleum.

There is a timelessness to the Fiore collection that makes it a strong investment. The name itself marries the Italian word fiore (meaning flower) with forever, and with this Bulgari offers flowers that will last a lifetime.

ABOVE: A high jewellery necklace with a Fiorever motif on display at Bulgari's Fifth Avenue store in New York.

Global Expansion

With a growing international client list, by 1970 it came time for Bulgari to set its sights on international expansion – starting in New York. The opening of a small store within the Pierre Hotel on the edge of Central Park would kickstart a rapid expansion drive for the Roman jeweller that would lead it to open stores and pick up stockists all over the world. This repositioning of Bulgari as a luxury brand would also lead to the development of new products. As well as jewellery and watches, it would launch perfumes, handbags and even dinner sets. Perhaps the most surprising brand extension of all would be its decision to enter the hotel business.

LEFT: A Bulgari store in the district of Ginza in Tokyo.

Becoming a Global Brand

Fresh off the back of its success during Rome's La Dolce Vita era, Bulgari set its sights on global expansion. Although Sortirio had experimented with a network of shops in the late 19th century, the brand had restricted itself to only having five stores in Italy. Though it had an international clientele, to step into a Bulgari boutique they must travel to its homeland.

This all changed in the 1970s. Under Gianni Bulgari's leadership, Bulgari opened stores in New York, Geneva, Monte Carlo and Paris.

In 1980, Bulgari set up Bulgari Distribuzione, a separate company that would design and manufacture goods to be sold though its growing global network of stores. This would help fuel a period of rapid expansion. Between 1986 and 1988 it would open stores in Milan, Tokyo, Hong Kong, Singapore, London, Saint-Moritz and New York.

During this time, it expanded its offering. Watches were becoming a more important part of the businesses, but it was also widening the scope of products it offered, to include perfumes, leather goods and silverware.

By 1995, Bulgari had 36 stores, 11 of which were run as franchises. It was also selling its perfume in 2,500 boutiques around the world, and had 120 stores selling its watches. In order to continue financing this expansion plan, Bulgari decided to go public with an IPO on the Milan Stock Exchange (Borsa Italiana) and London's SEAQ International for 36 per cent of its shares. The IPO sold out in two days, valuing the company at $383 million.

Bulgari was now the world's third-largest jewellery firm, hot on the heels of Cartier and Tiffany & Co.

OPPOSITE: A Serpenti installation at the Ginza, Tokyo, store, which is illuminated at night.

ABOVE: The Bulgari New York flagship, pictured in 2012 before its redesign.

New York

New York was the location of the brand's first international store since Sortirio's early expansion ended. The brand's products were already being sold in the US through an agent, but in 1972 it opened a boutique within the Pierre Hotel on the edge of Central Park.

In America, Bulgari positioned itself as luxury jewellery for women who wanted to have fun. It was tapping into the easy-going seventies zeitgeist. In a campaign starring the American singer Cher, Bulgari described its jewels as "real, but not too serious". In that campaign, Cher was wearing a collection called Stars and Stripes that Bulgari had created to celebrate the Pierre boutique opening. The collection used coral, lapis lazuli, enamel and diamonds to create stars

OPPOSITE: A Bulgari ring with diamonds, sapphires and rubies arranged as the American flag, which was worn by Nancy Reagan in 1986.

BELOW: When Bulgari closed its New York store to refurbish it, the brand covered it in a billboard with a quote from Andy Warhol.

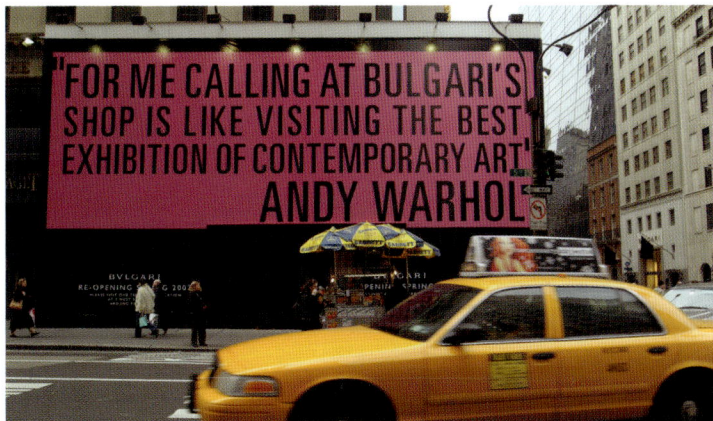

and stripes motifs in reference to the American flag.

Bulgari added pieces to the Stars and Stripes collection throughout the 1970s and into the early 1980s, but today it is a rare find on the secondary market, making it the holy grail for Bulgari collectors.

A special Stars and Stripes ring was made for former First Lady Nancy Reagan to wear at the centenary celebration of the Statue of Liberty. The flag on the gold ring was constructed with rubies, blue sapphires and diamonds. The ring came up for sale at Sotheby's in 2016 and fetched $319,000.

By the late 1980s, Bulgari had outgrown its Pierre Hotel boutique and moved to a larger location at 730 Fifth

Avenue. By now, Nicola Bulgari was living in New York, overseeing the American business, and making sure that he was part of all the right social circles.

The Fifth Avenue flagship opened in 1989, and the brand has remained there ever since. When Bulgari renewed the lease on the store in 2015, it set a new real-estate record for New York by paying a reported $5,000 per square foot.

To mark 40 years in the city, Bulgari called in its architect of choice, Peter Marino, to reimagine the space with a full refurbishment that would see the store close for 18 months before reopening in the winter of 2017. Marino's brief was to bring Rome to New York, and he has done so by mirroring many of the elements of the jeweller's Roman flagship on Via Condotti, including a reproduction of its iconic 1930s entrance, and drawing on a palate of gold and apricot inspired by sunny southern Italy.

While the original fascia in Rome is almost minimal in its chic use of neutral stonemasonry and marble window frames, New York is aggressive in its adornment. The exterior is caged in metal mesh inspired by the clasp of a 1930s bracelet. Each intersection is marked by floral Rosetta motifs fitted with 1,800 individually operated lights that can be used to create visual effects.

Visitors who cross the threshold will find themselves transported, by way of a star-patterned white Lasa marble mosaic, to a bright central promenade that is a gateway to a series of smaller, more intimate spaces. Each pays homage to Italian culture and the brand's glamorous history, including a VIP area named after Bulgari superfan Elizabeth Taylor.

OPPOSITE: The Fifth Avenue store after the 2017 refurbishment led by Peter Marino.

LEFT: A shopper walks by a window display at the New York flagship store.

Pierre Robbery

During Bulgari's stay at the Pierre Hotel, a crime took place that had a rather unusual ending. On 19th January, 1977, a conman called Peter N. Lazaros, who police once described as a "one-man crime wave", checked into a suite at the Pierre Hotel. He called down to the Bulgari store, posing as a potential customer, and asked for a selection of rings to be brought to his suite.

The Bulgari team obliged. After Lazaros was shown the rings, he rejected them all and sent the salespeople away. However, on returning to the store, they realised that a ring was missing. It was a platinum design set with two emerald-cut diamonds weighing a combined 4cts, and was valued at $35,000. The police were alerted, but by the time the crime was realised, the conman had escaped with the ring. The Bulgari store would get the ring back a year later – but in the strangest of circumstances.

Lazaros had died in April 1978 in Pontiac, Michigan, and when his body was sent for autopsy, the pathologist discovered the ring in his small intestine. As it was stamped with the Bvlgari logo, the FBI were able to trace it back to Bulgari and return the ring.

OPPOSITE: The Pierre, an iconic hotel on East 61st Street at Fifth Avenue in New York City.

The Bulgari Lifestyle

For those who have bought into the Bulgari brand,
it has always been about so much more than simply
acquiring a piece of jewellery, or a watch. It is
also about tapping into the glamour and Italian
exuberance that the name carries. To cater to those
wishing for a little slice of La Dolce Vita, Bulgari
tried out new product lines as it began to morph into
a lifestyle brand.

An early hit in the 1970s was the Melone bag, a solid
18ct gold fluted oval clutch bag with diamond-set
clasp and a decorative tassel. Such was the fervour
for this luxury accessory, some of which were further
decorated with gemstone inlay, that there was a
waiting list. Today, Bulgari Melone bags sell on the
secondary market for tens of thousands of pounds.
Later, in 1979, Bulgari began to produce silver
household objects, such as vases and bookmarks.

These early items were still very tied to jewellery,
being made of precious metals, but in 1990 a new era
of branding erupted as Bulgari moved into perfume,
setting up Bulgari Parfums in Neuchâtel, Switzerland.

After two years of research and development,
it launched is first fragrance, Eau Parfumée au
Thé Vert, which was masterminded by respected
perfumer Jean-Claude Ellena. The top notes were
Italian bergamot, Spanish orange blossom, Ceylon
cardamom, Jamaican pepper and Russian coriander.

OPPOSITE: Bulgari perfumes on display in Sabiha
Gökçen International Airport, Istanbul.

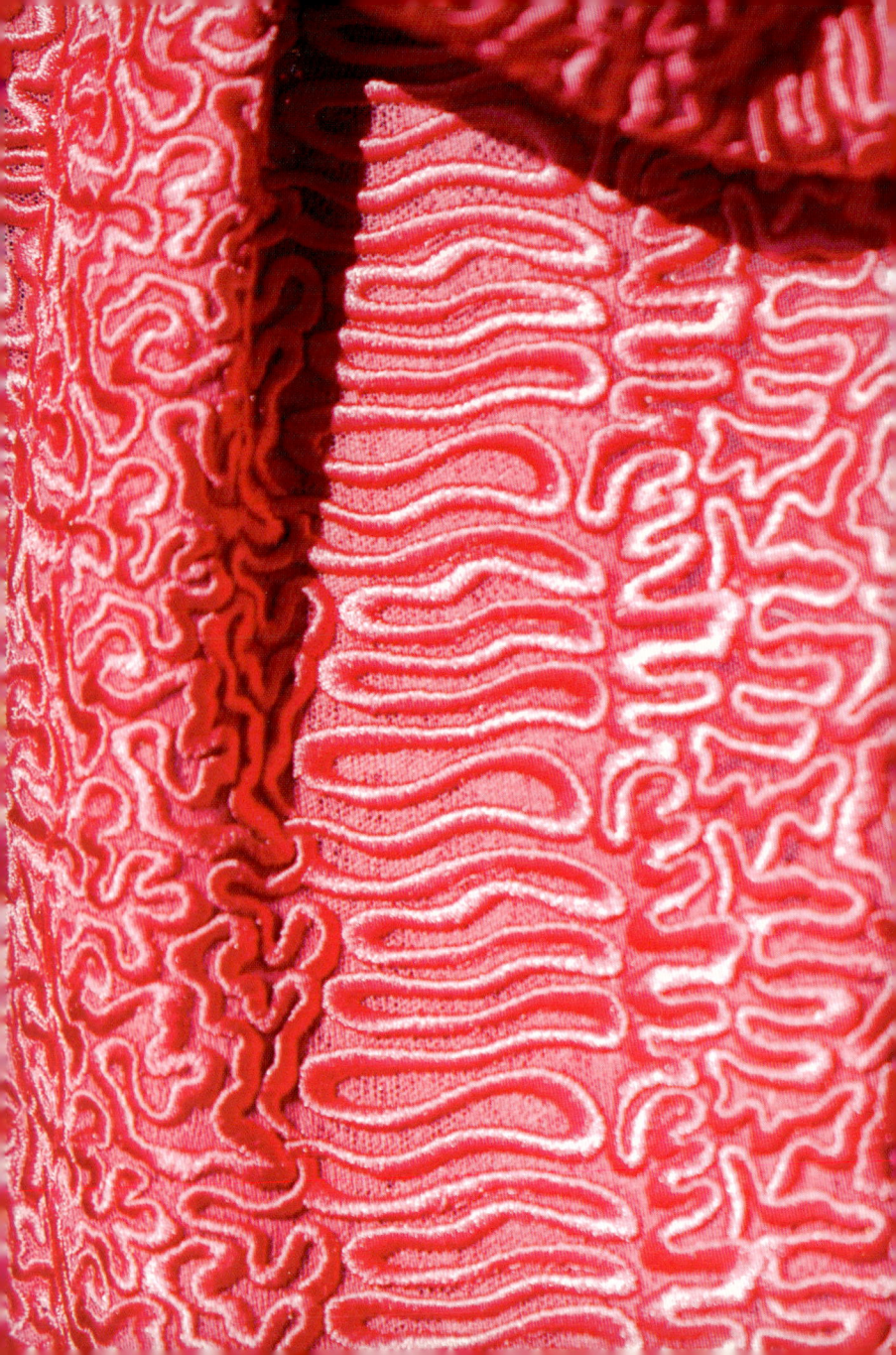

The mid notes were Bulgarian rose and Egyptian jasmine. The base notes were green tea and smoked wood. The effect was a fresh, androgynous citrus scent.

Bulgari launched many more fragrances after this, and the Bvlgari branding became a common sight in many fragrance outlets across the world. As well as developing signature scents, a lot of effort went into creating the elaborate bottles that hold them.

Eyewear was next. In 1997, global eyewear manufacturer Luxottica purchased the licensing rights to create a line of Bulgari sunglasses and spectacles. The design of these luxury accessories take inspiration from Bulgari jewellery collections including Serpenti and B.zero1.

In 1998, Bulgari added a new string to its bow: a line of tableware. In an interview with the *Financial Times* that year, Bulgari chief executive Francesco Trapani said Bulgari was modelling itself on Cartier, with regards to the breadth of lifestyle products it would offer. "Soon, we will have the same portfolio of products as Cartier with the exception that we sell ties, they don't, and they sell cigarettes and we don't," he said.

Contemporary lines of ties offer bold colours, with some designs inspired by Serpenti scales, or creating patterns from the Bvlgari logo, and there is a gold-tone tie clip in the shape of a "B" within the collection. The brand also produces a line of silk and cashmere scarves.

In 2008, Bulgari set up an accessories workshop in Florence dedicated to handcrafting its handbags. It is based in an old textile mill on the Arno river; the location was chosen for its proximity to the world's top tanneries. Many of the bags draw inspiration from the Serpenti motif, with snake-head clasps or serpentine handles. Bulgari has also collaborated with designers including Mary Katrantzou and Ambush to create their own twist on Serpenti bags. Katrantzou was later appointed the brand's first-ever creative director of leather goods in 2024.

PREVIOUS: A white leather Serpenti bag with a snakehead clasp, as seen at Milan Fashion Week, 2017.

OPPOSITE: A black leather Serpenti bag displayed in a store window in Paris.

RIGHT: A woman wears a pair of Bulgari sunglasses at Milan Fashion Week, 2015.

Hotels

Bulgari was fast becoming not just a world-famous jeweller and watchmaker, but a global lifestyle brand, and in 2001 it made a rather unexpected move. The jeweller turned hotelier. Its hotel brand Bulgari Hotels & Resorts was launched as a joint venture with Luxury Group, a division of global hotel giant Marriott International, which is also responsible for the five-star Ritz-Carlton hotels.

The joint venture was reported at the time to be an investment to the tune of $140 million, with Bulgari taking a 65 per cent stake and Marriott International a 35 per cent stake. Bulgari chief executive Francesco Trapani said that the driver behind the launch of the hotels business was to make the Bulgari name even more widely known as a signum of luxury.

The first Bulgari hotel opened in Milan on 18th May, 2004, on Via Privata Fratelli Gabba in the city's chic Brera neighbourhood. The 58-room hotel is situated next to the Botanical Gardens and set at the centre of a 4,000sqm private garden, of which each room has a view.

Walk through the hotel, and you will be reminded of its owners. Sketches of Giardinetto brooches from the 1950s hang on the landings, and photographs of celebrities in Bulgari jewels line the lobby. Each hotel room also has framed sketches of magnificent jewels. As well as accommodation, the hotel has a restaurant, bar, private dining room, spa and cigar room. The idea was that this should not just be a bolthole for hotel guests but a social destination for locals.

To reach the Milan hotel, you must enter a private road, and this balance of tranquillity in the busy city has become a hallmark of Bulgari Hotels as the network has grown. In London, the hotel is on one of Knightsbridge's quieter side streets, and in Shanghai it is in a protected heritage zone in the Jing'an district.

All of the hotels have a sense of uniformity to them, as you would expect from any hotel group. As well as the sketches and photographs boasting Bulgari's bejewelled heritage, there are subtler touchpoints: the use of marble, eight-pointed stars stitched into curtains in a nod to its New York flagship exterior, and in the Paris outpost there are glass panels depicting serpents in the bathrooms.

By 2024, there were nine Bulgari hotels: Milan, London, Dubai, Bali, Beijing, Shanghai, Paris, Tokyo and Rome. There were also plans to open locations in the Maldives in 2025, and Los Angeles and Miami in 2026.

The 2023 opening of the Bulgari hotel in Rome was a particularly special moment for the brand, seeing as it is the city where the jeweller's story really began. The hotels team had spent a decade searching for the right location in the Eternal City. They found it at 10 Piazza Augusto Imperatore in the heart of the city, opposite legendary Roman landmark the Mausoleum of Augustus.

The 14,000sqm hotel was created by architect Vittorio Ballio Morpurgo and is a celebration of Rome's history. A marble statue of the emperor Augustus, borrowed from the famous Fondazione Torlonia collection, greets visitors at the entrance. Other luxurious heritage touches within the Rome hotel include hand-crafted mosaics inspired by Bulgari motifs, Murano glass light fittings and 1930s Ginori vases.

Celebrity Fans

Celebrity endorsement plays a key role in Bulgari's ascension to becoming a major player on the world stage. In La Dolce Vita days, it was stars of the silver screen buying and wearing its jewels that got it noticed. In contemporary times, however, aligning with star power is a little more transactional.

Bulgari collections – especially its bold, colourful cabochons and the sinuous Serpenti jewels – are often seen on the red carpet, most often worn by its ambassadors. Bulgari has had many famous faces associated with the brand over the years, including Zendaya, Bella Hadid, Jessica Chastain, Naomi Watts and Selena Gomez.

It was reported by Page Six that model Cara Delevigne was paid £200,000 to wear Bulgari jewellery to the 2023 Academy Awards. The star wore a magnificent

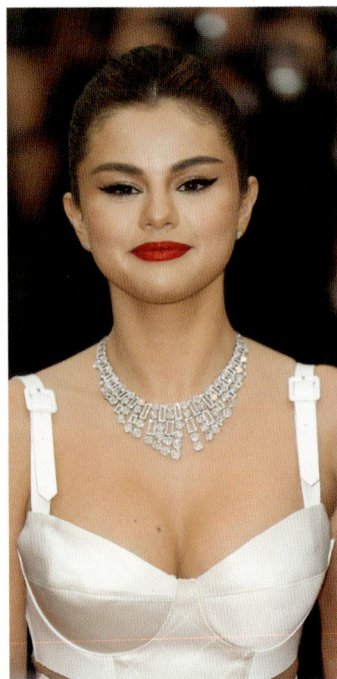

three-strand diamond Serpenti choker, a Serpenti bracelet, Serpenti ear clips and a diamond ring. She paired these all-white jewels with a one-shouldered red dress by Elie Saab.

Regardless of the backroom deals required to get jewels on the red carpet, Bulgari's regular appearances keep its jewels and name at the forefront of our minds.

OPPOSITE TOP: Naomi Watts wears a Bulgari necklace during the 2016 Cannes Film Festival.

ABOVE: Jessica Chastain wears a Serpenti necklace during the Toronto International Film Festival, 2023.

OPPOSITE BOTTOM: Selena Gomez in a diamond Bulgari necklace at the 2019 Cannes Film Festival.

OPPOSITE: Zendaya wears Bulgari jewellery to the Annual Screen Actors Guild Awards in 2023.

RIGHT: Stylist Law Roach wears a Bulgari Giardinetto brooch to the Fashion Trust US Awards in 2023.

BELOW LEFT: Bella Hadid wears a Serpenti bracelet and Bulgari earrings during the 2018 Cannes Film Festival.

BELOW RIGHT: Cara Delevigne in a Serpenti choker and earrings at the Academy Awards in 2023.

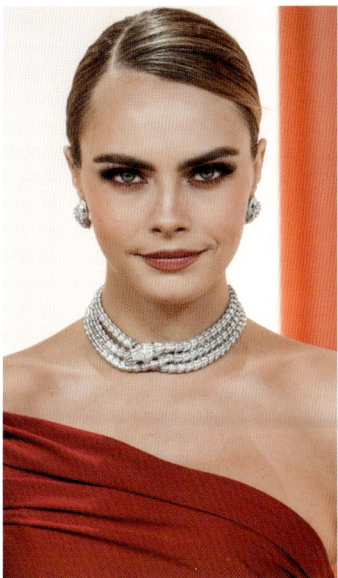

Legacy

Creating a luxury brand is one thing, but protecting it and ensuring its future is entirely another. Bulgari has taken many measures to ensure that its name remains synonymous with Italian glamour, from shoring up its archives and buying back important jewels to hosting exhibitions.

It is also important to note the legacy that the brand and the family has left beyond its own collections. Many of the Bulgari family have gone on to start other creative projects, while Bulgari's philanthropic work has improved lives and saved many Ancient Roman monuments. It has also made a commitment to protecting the crafts that it relies on by educating and nurturing a new generation of talent.

RIGHT: A yellow gold and diamond Serpenti necklace.

The Bulgari Family

The Bulgari family – or the Voulgaris – have been central to the story of Italy's most famous jeweller. They are a luxury dynasty, and their influence has spread far beyond the original brand.

Many of the Bulgaris have gone on to work on other projects within the jewellery world. One of the first to leave the family firm was Marina Bulgari. After exiting her role at Bulgari in 1976 – citing irreconcilable differences with her cousins Paolo, Gianni and Nicola – she set up her own jewellery brand. Unable to use the family name of Bulgari due to legal reasons, she settled on Marina B.

Her brand's style was not too dissimilar to Bulgari's: voluminous, bold, colourful. It also produced many tubogas jewels. Marina B opened its first store in Geneva in 1978, followed by New York in 1986 and Paris in 1987. More stores would open in Milan and Rome, and the brand picked up a celebrity following –

including many stars who were fans of Bulgari, such as Elizabeth Taylor and Sophia Loren.

In 1999, Marina B was bought by the Saudi Arabian sheikh Ahmed Fitaihi, but the company would pass through more hands. It was bought by Windsor Jewels in 2010, Paul Lubetsky in 2014, and Guy Bedarida in 2017. By the time Bedarida took over, Marina had retired to Monte Carlo, and on Valentine's Day 2024, aged 93, Marina passed away.

OPPOSITE: Nicola Bulgari attending The Rodeo Drive Walk Of Style event held to honour Bulgari in 2012.

ABOVE: Marina Bulgari at an exhibition of her jewellery in Geneva, Switzerland, in 2003.

Fiery family politics would also cause Gianni to leave Bulgari in 1987. He had fallen out with Paolo and Nicola, and allowed them to buy him out of the business. Gianni – a keen sportsman – made a pivot to the fashion world at that point, and was appointed chairman of sportswear brand Fila in 1988, where he would stay for a decade. Alongside this role, he also founded a Swiss watchmaking company called GB Enigma, which launched in 1989. One of its most original designs was the 1997 BMW (Bazel Manual Winder), a mechanical watch that could be wound by turning the bezel.

Gianni's son Giorgio Bulgari – named for his grandfather – would also follow in his family's footsteps. Giorgio was raised in New York and later settled in Geneva, where he worked in finance before joining his father in the luxury business. He had a flair for design, and collaborated with fashion house Salvatore Ferragamo on its first jewellery line. Giorgio then spent four years as creative director at his aunt's brand, Marina B.

In 2017, Giorgio decided to strike out on his own. Like his aunt, he could not use his family name for legal reasons, so adopted the same tactic as her by launching as Giorgio B. He spent the first seven years as a private jeweller, making bespoke, one-of-a-kind commissions to order. Then in 2023, he introduced collections.

Giorgio B jewellery encapsulates some of the bold stylings of his family style, but it very much has its own signature. Giorgio favours bold but smooth silhouettes that rely on metal and enamel rather than gems, although his bespoke high jewellery commissions do use top-quality gemstones. The collections, which are akin to wearable contemporary art, have attracted the gaze of the rich and the famous – just like those of his ancestors.

ABOVE: Sharon Stone wears Giorgio B earrings
to the 2023 *Vanity Fair* Oscars Party.

LVMH Sale

It was the beginning of the end of an era in 2011 when the last remaining Bulgari family members struck a deal to give control of the business to LVMH. The family remained involved, but the luxury conglomerate became the major shareholder for the price of €3.7 billion.

It had been a tough few years for Bulgari since the 2008 financial crisis. That year, its net profits fell 45 per cent, forcing it to cut jobs, close stores and reduce inventory. In 2009, Francesco, as chief executive, took a 75 per cent pay cut.

Less than a year after the LVMH deal was struck, Paolo, Nicola and Francesco sold their remaining stake, which was worth €558 million. Bulgari was left without any Bulgaris, although the family would often turn up for events and publicity shots, and Francesco joined LVMH as head of watches and jewellery until 2014.

Under the new ownership, Bulgari flourished. By 2015, it had expanded its store portfolio to 300, and benefitted from an ambitious and gregarious new CEO in Jean-Christophe Babin. Despite the family no longer shaping its story, Bulgari remains one of the largest and most influential jewellery brands in the world.

ABOVE: Bulgari was bought by luxury group LVMH in 2011.

Bulgari Manifattura Valenza

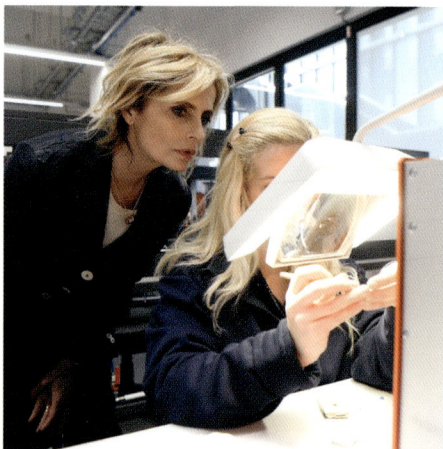

"Made in Italy" carries a lot of weight around the world, and it is a manufacturing standard that Bulgari upholds. Its leather goods are made in Florence, its perfumes in Lodi, its silk scarves in Como, and its high jewellery in Rome.

As the Bulgari brand expanded, there became a need for increased manufacturing capabilities, and in 2017 it opened a 14,000sqm manufacturing site in Valenza. The city is a well-known goldsmithing hub, so it was the perfect choice for the location of the Bulgari Manifattura. The site, which created an additional 300 jobs when it opened, spans two buildings. The first is the Cascina dell'Orefice, a site at which goldsmiths have been practicing their craft since the early 19th century. Bulgari expanded this building by adding a new wing encased entirely in glass that it calls the Glass House. The second building has three floors, set around a 600sqm interior courtyard that allows light to flow in.

Sustainability was taken into consideration when making this new facility. Integrated initiatives include solar power, water filtration and reclamation, and an external "skin" that keeps the building cool on hot Italian days.

This green approach to the build and running of the facility led it to be awarded the LEED (Leadership in Energy and Environmental Design) Gold Certification, an international symbol of sustainability.

The building holds 18 jewellery-making workshops and two training workshops. Bulgari claims it to be the largest jewellery manufacturing complex in Europe. It is a centre for learning as well as production, as the Bulgari Jewellery Academy is based here, and in its inaugural year it had capacity for 42 students.

OPPOSITE: Italian actress Isabella Ferrari attends the Bulgari Manifattura opening on 17th March, 2017, in Valenza, Italy.

ABOVE: Guests including Nicola Bulgari (centre, left), Isabella Ferrari (centre), and Jean-Christophe Babin (centre, right) at the cutting of the ribbon of the Bulgari Manifattura.

Protecting the Craft

The Bulgari Jewellery Academy is part of the Italian jeweller's drive to protect the handcrafts it relies on to make its jewels, by pairing masters with apprentices. There, skilled Bulgari craftspeople show students how to perfect the skills required to make the brand's signature jewellery.

Bulgari estimates that its Academy provides 130,000 hours of training a year, delivered by its master goldsmiths, gem setters and polishers. The Academy is a strong source of new talent for the jeweller, with Bulgari retaining nine out of 10 new hires who have passed through the training.

In Switzerland, there is another Bulgari Academy – this time dedicated to watchmaking. Again, the development of the Bulgari Watches Academy is led by a desire to attract and retain new talent. The centre deals with two types of training: apprenticeships for people who are new to the industry and continuous employee learning.

The brand is also a part of LVMH's Institut des Métiers d'Excellence (IME) Initiative. This apprenticeship programme helps to train young people aged 18 to 29 to develop careers in the luxury industry, with 78 per cent continuing their studies or finding jobs that call for the skills they have learned at the IME.

Bulgari has also partnered with external schools and universities, including Central Saint Martins in London and Scuola Superiore Sant'Anna in Pisa, to work on collaborative projects or give students an insight into the business.

OPPOSITE: A craftsperson works on a high jewellery necklace at Bulgari's workshop in Rome.

LEFT: Gemstones are laid out, ready to be set into a necklace at the Bulgari workshop in Rome.

Philanthropy

As with the majority of global brands, philanthropy is core to Bulgari's activities. One of its most famous charity collaborations has been with Save the Children. The partnership started in 2009 with the launch of a dedicated jewellery line to raise money for the charity. The jewels are based on its popular B.zero1 line but are crafted in silver, and therefore more accessibly priced than the main gold B.zero1 range. The jewels – which include rings, pendants and bracelets – feature the Bvlgari Bvlgari logo as well as a Save the Children logo. Some have hidden red enamel details or a ruby to tie in with the charity's brand colours.

The campaign has garnered a lot of celebrity support since its launch, with more than 250 celebrities becoming ambassadors. Many of them have been shot by world-famous photographer Fabrizio Ferri while wearing the Save the Children jewels. Often, they will hold their hands aloft as a symbol of the campaign's message: Stop. Think. Give. In the first 12 years of the partnership, Bulgari raised $100 million for Save the Children, with the charity estimating that the funding has touched the lives of more than

OPPOSITE: Actors Naomi Watts and Adrien Brody and photographer Fabrizio Ferri attend a Save The Children event hosted by Bulgari in Beverly Hills, California, in 2015.

LEFT: Bulgari ambassadors Jordi Molla and Hiba Abouk visit a new centre for children at risk of social exclusion in Madrid in 2017.

BELOW: Actor Julian Sands attends the Bulgari and Save the Children event in Beverly Hills, California, in 2015.

2 million children. Part of the money raised has been used to train 73,000 teachers in 37 countries around the world.

Another important initiative for Bulgari is the Avrora Awards, which celebrate women excelling in their chosen field. The Awards, launched in 2016 in Japan, are named after the Roman goddess of dawn, Aurora (Bulgari tweaked the name to incorporate its brand signature "V").

The Awards recognise women working in a number of fields, including film, music, arts, craftsmanship, business, CSR, sports and research. The awards are regional, with editions taking place in Japan, China, South Korea and Europe.

In 2020, Bulgari launched a new programme designed to support women in the sciences. The Bulgari Women & Science Fellowship Fund provided female scientists at the Rockefeller University in New York with funding to undertake scientific research to combat the Covid-19 pandemic and advance virology and immunology studies.

Bulgari did a lot of work during the pandemic to help advance science and protect people. In addition to the Women & Science Fellowship Fund, it established a separate Clinical Fund to finance the development and testing of vaccines, and made a donation to the Spallanzani Hospital in Rome. It also converted its fragrance factory to produce hand sanitising gel, donating more than 160,000 bottles to NHS workers in the UK and medical facilities in Switzerland and Italy.

OPPOSITE TOP: Bulgari CEO Jean-Christophe Babin, actor Hilary Swank, de Young Museum president Dede Wilsey and Nicola Bulgari attend the Art Of Bulgari event held at the de Young Museum in San Francisco in 2013.

RIGHT: Michelle Francine Ngonmo, Boris Barboni, Lucia Silvestri, Sharon Stone, Kylie Minogue, Little Simz, Veronica Yoko Plebani, Jean-Christophe Babin, Anna Osei, and Rita Ora attend the 2022 Avrora Awards in Milan.

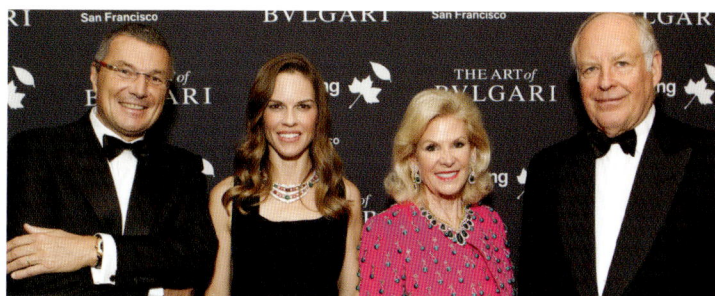

Rebuilding Rome

Bulgari is endlessly inspired by Rome, and to pay its respects to the city that has been its home and its muse, the jeweller is involved in a number of restoration projects.

It started in 2014 with the Spanish Steps – a Roman landmark that is visible from its Via Condotti store. Indeed, when Bulgari first had three stores in the city, it was these steps that connected them. It donated €1.5 million to help the Municipality of Rome maintain the steps. The money funded cleaning and repairs, as well as the restoration of 16 iron lampposts and the modernising of the lighting system with LED bulbs.

Next on the list was the Caracalla Baths, which is said to be the finest example of an ancient Roman bath in the city, boasting with masterful mosaics. Bulgari sponsored restoration work at the Baths, including revealing floor mosaics that had been hidden for more than 40 years.

Another restoration partnership that Bulgari entered into was with Fondazione Torlonia, which controls a private collection of classic statues. Together, the organisations have restored more than 90 Greek and Roman statues.

Funding from Bulgari also facilitated an international tour of the statues. Guests at the Bulgari Hotel in Rome will be able to see some of this work up close, as the hotel lobby is host to a statue from the Fondazione Torlonia.

Other restoration projects have followed, and Bulgari is responsible for preserving many more Roman monuments. In 2019, it funded relighting the Ara Pacis, an altar that dates back to 9BC and was created to welcome Augustus, Rome's first emperor, back to the city after three years away. It also helped to make the four Roman temples of Area Sacra di Largo Arentina in Rome accessible to the public for the first time.

OPPOSITE: The Spanish Steps in Rome.

BELOW: Relief of a goddess with twin babies on the Ara Pacis in Rome.

Exhibitions

Protecting Bulgari's legacy is as much about looking back as it is preparing for the future, which is why the brand has a very active Historical Archive. The Archives team catalogues information about Bulgari, but it also collects real jewels. The team is charged with collecting strong examples of Bulgari craftsmanship from all eras of its history. Some might be bought back at auction – like Elizabeth Taylor's pieces – or direct from clients. The brand has been known to run adverts in newspapers to let collectors know that it is seeking jewels in a certain style, or from a particular era.

Often, it can be incredibly hard to win these jewels back, especially the rarer items. Lucia Bosciana, former heritage curator at Bulgari, once described it as "mission impossible". For those that have been found, they serve many purposes: to inspire the design team, to be worn on the red carpet by celebrities, and to be displayed in exhibitions.

Curating and taking part in exhibitions is incredibly important to Bulgari. It has hosted many themed exhibitions, and also has a permanent exhibition space at 10 Via Condotti in Rome to showcase pieces from its Heritage collection. This museum of jewellery is open every day and is free to visit.

Bulgari also collaborates with other creatives on exhibitions. To mark the 75th anniversary of its Serpenti design, Bulgari teamed up with digital artist Refik Anadol to create an immersive experience that was hosted in Milan and London. Anadol used AI to create an undulating, serpentine digital artwork called *Serpenti Metamorphosis* that was created by feeding an AI programme more than 200 million images of nature. It was projected into an enclosed space, with viewers required to walk into a box to experience it. The artwork was multi-sensory, with a nature-inspired soundtrack and rainforest-inspired scent, both of which were created by AI.

OPPOSITE: Guests view Refik Anadol's Serpenti-inspired AI-generated art at an exhibition to mark 75 years of the iconic Bulgari design at the Museum of Contemporary Art in Shanghai, China, in 2023.

Eternal Appeal

Bulgari, the jeweller that rose from the streets of Rome – Italy's Eternal City – has created a legacy that has its own eternal appeal.

The distinctive style of jewellery it has created has set it apart from other major luxury groups. There is nothing reserved about Bulgari. Whether it is creating a lavishly colourful piece of high jewellery or yet another record-breaking watch, it approaches everything it does with gusto.

Underpinning all of this, however, is a deep commitment to craftsmanship. This ensures that, in addition to exciting collectors with its often provocative designs, the collector trusts that the creator has made something that will last a lifetime – and beyond.

The brand's enduring appeal also lies in its ability to seamlessly blend tradition with innovation. Bulgari continually pushes the boundaries of design, introducing

OPPOSITE: A shopper walks past a Bulgari window display on Via dei Condotti, Rome.

ABOVE: A Diva's Dream installation at the New York flagship.

OVERLEAF: The famous marble architraves of the Via dei Condotti store in Rome.

ground-breaking techniques and materials while staying true to its heritage. This fusion of classic elegance and contemporary style resonates with discerning clientele worldwide. You can see the eternal appeal of Bulgari in action when you look to the secondary market, where exceptional Bulgari pieces can sell for hundreds of thousands of pounds.

Furthermore, Bulgari's association with glamour and celebrity has contributed to its timeless allure. From Hollywood stars to royalty, Bulgari's creations have adorned some of the world's most iconic figures, cementing its status as a symbol of luxury and prestige.

In essence, Bulgari's eternal appeal lies in its ability to transcend time and trends. It is this perfect balance of tradition, innovation and elegance that continues to captivate and enchant aficionados around the globe.

Image Credits

Page 5 REPORT/Shutterstock; 7 luca85/Shutterstock; 8 Bulgari; 11 Bulgari; 12 courtesy of Sotheby's; 13 courtesy of Sotheby's; 14 Archive PL/Alamy; 15 Shawshots/Alamy; 17 courtesy of Sotheby's; 18-19 courtesy of Sotheby's; 20 Casimiro PT/Shutterstock; 23 Bulgari; 24 Obs70 Shutterstock; 25 K - Photo/Shutterstock; 26-27 Claudio Stocco/Shutterstock; 28 MonikaKL/Shutterstock; 29 MonikaKL/Shutterstock; 30 Sipa US/Alamy; 32 Associated Press/Alamy; 33 Penta Springs Limited/Alamy; 34 courtesy of Sotheby's; 37 courtesy of Sotheby's; 39 LANDMARK MEDIA/Alamy; 40 SilverScreen/Alamy; 41 Pictorial Press Ltd/Alamy; 42 (t) Associated Press/Alamy; 42 (b) Photo 12/Alamy; 43 Keystone Press/Alamy; 45 (l) INTERFOTO/Alamy; 45 (r) Mondadori Portfolio/Getty; 46 PictureLux/The Hollywood Archive/Alamy; 47 (l) FlixPix/Alamy; 47 (r) PA Images/Alamy; 48 Archivio TV Sorrisi e Canzoni/Bridgeman Images; 49 Everett Collection Inc/Alamy; 51 Retro AdArchives/Alamy; 52 courtesy of Sotheby's; 53 Peregrine/Alamy; 54 Peter Horree/Alamy; 55 (t) ZUMA Press, Inc/Alamy; 55 (b) PSL Images/Alamy; 56 Retro AdArchives/Alamy; 59 Sipa US/Alamy; 60 Yaroslaff/Shutterstock; 61 Everett Collection Inc/Alamy; 62 WWD/Getty; 63 Associated Press/Alamy; 65 Eric VANDEVILLE/Getty; 66 Keystone Press/Alamy; 67 Associated Press/Alamy; 68 Creative Lab/Shutterstock; 70

yu_photo/Shutterstock; 71 Patti McConville/Alamy; 73 Serge Mouraret/Alamy; 74 Bloomberg/Getty; 76 Robb Report/Getty; 77 (l) Graphic Gang/Shutterstock; 77 (r) Matthew Bain Inc/Shutterstock; 79 Patti McConville/Alamy; 80 A. Astes/Alamy; 81 Associated Press/Alamy; 83 Image Press Agency/Alamy; 85 courtesy of Sotheby's; 86 Patti McConville/Alamy; 88 A. Astes/Alamy; 89 Patti McConville/Alamy; 91 courtesy of Sotheby's; 93 ZUMA Press, Inc/Alamy; 95 Massimo Salesi/Shutterstock; 96 courtesy of Sotheby's; 99 (t) dpa picture alliance/Alamy; 99 (b) Art of Life/Shutterstock; 101 yu_photo/Shutterstock; 102 Grzegorz Czapsk/Alamy; 104 courtesy of Sotheby's; 107 Patti McConville/Alamy; 108 Michael Gordon/Shutterstock; 110 Lina Sariff/Shutterstock; 111 DW Labs Incorporated/Shutterstock; 112 dpa picture alliance/Alamy; 113 Richard Levine/Alamy; 114 christianthiel.net/Shutterstock; 115 Alfonso Lozano del Rey/Shutterstock; 117 Kenneth Grant/Alamy; 119 Firat Cetin/Shutterstock; 120-121 andersphoto/Shutterstock; 122 Ms Egoroff/Shutterstock; 123 andersphoto/Shutterstock; 126 Ritu Manoj Jethani/Shutterstock; 127 Abaca Press/Alamy; 128 (t) magicinfoto/Shutterstock; 128 (b) Abaca Press/Alamy; 129 Associated Press/Alamy; 130 Sipa US/Alamy; 131 (t) ZUMA Press, Inc./Alamy; 131 (bl) magicinfoto/Shutterstock; 131 (br) Sipa US/Alamy; 133 ANGHI/Shutterstock; 134 ZUMA Press, Inc./

RIGHT: A Serpenti necklace on display at a Bulgari store in Paris.

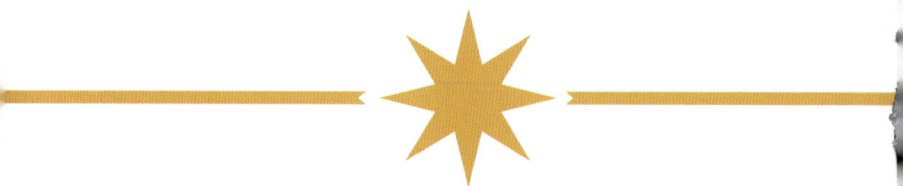